SETTING A
TRAP
FOR
GOD

The Aramaic
Prayer Of Jesus

Also by Rocco A. Errico

Let There Be Light: The Seven Keys
Treasures From the Language of Jesus
The Mysteries of Creation: The Genesis Story
The Message of Matthew: An Annotated Parallel
Aramaic-English Gospel of Matthew
Classical Aramaic (Grammar Book 1)
Classical Aramaic (Grammar Book 2)
La antigua oración aramea de Jesús: El Padrenuestro

Rocco A. Errico

SETTING A
TRAP

FOR

GOD

The Aramaic
Prayer Of Jesus

UNITY®
Books

Unity Village, MO

New Edition 1997

Setting a Trap for God: The Aramaic Prayer of Jesus, has been revised and expanded. It was originally published as *The Ancient Aramaic Prayer of Jesus: The Lord's Prayer,* copyright © 1975 by Noohra Foundation (formerly Aramaic Bible Center).

To receive a catalog of all Unity products or to place an order, call the Customer Care Department at 1-800-669-0282 or visit *www.unity.org.* Unity Books are available at special discounts for bulk purchases for study groups, book clubs, sales promotions, book signings or fundraising. To place a bulk order, call the Customer Care Department at 866-236-3571 or email *wholesaleaccts@unityonline.org.*

The Lamsa translation quotations in this book are reprinted by permission of Harper & Row Publishers, Inc., from *Holy Bible From the Ancient Eastern Text,* George M. Lamsa's translations from the Aramaic of the Peshitta. Copyright © 1933; renewed 1961 by Nina Shabaz. Copyright © 1939; renewed 1967 by Nina Shabaz. Copyright © 1940; renewed 1968 by Nina Shabaz. Copyright © 1957 by Nina Shabaz.

Cover design by Myra Colbert

LIBRARY OF CONGRESS CATALOGING-IN-PUBLICATION DATA
Errico, Rocco A.
    Setting a trap for God : the Aramaic prayer of Jesus / Rocco A. Errico. — Rev. and expanded.
      p. cm.
    Revision of: The Aramaic prayer of Jesus.
    Includes bibliographical references.
    ISBN 0-87159-124-3
    978-0-87159-124-1
    1. Lord's prayer. I. Errico, Rocco A. Aramaic prayer of Jesus. II. Title.
BV230.E75   1997
226.9'6077—dc20
                                   96-20661
                                      CIP

Canada GST R132529033

To
the Reverend Johnnie Colemon, Ph.D.,
of Christ Universal Temple, Chicago, Illinois.
As a token of my deepest and sincerest appreciation
for the many years of friendship and
faithfulness to the Aramaic work,
I dedicate this book.

Acknowledgments

I am deeply grateful to and appreciative of several individuals. I especially wish to acknowledge the Reverend Richard L. Hill, vice president of the Noohra Foundation, for his continual editorial recommendations and constructive criticisms.

I also wish to express my thanks to Ms. Sue Edwards, Ms. Nell Clement, and Ms. Linetta Izenman for their helpful comments and suggestions.

NOTE: The ancient Aramaic symbol which appears on the opening chapter pages of this book is a scribal abbreviation of the name of God: *Yah* for *Yahweh*. Near Eastern Assyrian Christian scribes usually placed the *Yah* at the beginning of a holy book and on the first page of a sacred writing or manuscript.

Table of Contents

Abbreviations

Gen. . . . . Genesis
Ex. . . . . Exodus
Num. . . . . Numbers
Deut. . . . . Deuteronomy
Ps. . . . . Psalms
Prov. . . . . Proverbs
Jer. . . . . Jeremiah
NT . . . . New Testament
Mt. . . . . Matthew
Mk. . . . . Mark
Lk. . . . . Luke
Jn. . . . . John
Rom. . . . . Romans
1 Cor. . . . . 1 Corinthians
Col. . . . . Colossians
Jas. . . . . James
1 Jn. . . . . 1 John
KJV . . . . King James Version
C.E. . . . . Common Era (A.D.)

Preface to New Edition

My book entitled *The Lord's Prayer* was first published in 1975. Then in 1978, with a slight revision, the book was republished under the title of *The Ancient Aramaic Prayer of Jesus: The Lord's Prayer.* Now, in 1997, it is with great pleasure that I present this new edition of Jesus' prayer entitled *Setting a Trap for God: The Aramaic Prayer of Jesus.* It is totally revised and expanded.

Why This Book Is Different

Over the centuries many authors have written volumes on this well-known prayer of Jesus. This book, however, approaches each line of the prayer directly from the ancient, biblical Aramaic tongue. When the great Nazarene prophet and wisdom teacher first taught his short prayer to his young students and to the Aramaic-speaking people of Galilee, he uttered it in his own native tongue, Aramaic. Later, the prayer appeared in written form in the gospels of Matthew (Mt. 6:9-13) and Luke (Lk. 11:2-4). The most common and accepted form of the prayer is the one recorded in Matthew. This book works with Jesus' prayer as we find it in his gospel text. Matthew's narrative is the first book we encounter in the New Testament. Many scholars think that Matthew wrote his gospel originally in Aramaic.

The Purpose of This Book

The purpose of this volume is to give the reader a new perspective and broader understanding of the basic significance of Jesus' famous prayer. It explains in ordinary and nontheological terminology, the meaning of the Aramaic words that Jesus spoke. It also clarifies what the words meant to his disciples and followers then, and what these words hold for us today. Through the Aramaic language, we learn how to apply Jesus' method of prayer for practical everyday living.

The Aramaic prayer of Jesus contains eight attunements that align us with spiritual forces in and around us. This book shows us how the Galilean Master Teacher taught his disciples to tap into the inexhaustible source and power he called *abba*, "Father." This Source has always been accessible for everyone in every age. It is the way of health, peace, prosperity, and enlightenment.

However, Jesus often seems to many readers of the New Testament to be an idealist rather than a pragmatist. But, the opposite is true. He was a down-to-earth, practical teacher.

What has been standing in our way of understanding Jesus' message more clearly is the Semitic, religio-cultural language that he used. (In reality, this is the problem we face with the entire New Testament.) This book helps us to break through that religio- cultural language barrier. It is a look into the Semitic world of two thousand years ago, bringing that ancient wisdom into our modern times. Jesus' prayer is the ideal path for us to enter his Semitic world.

The Question of God's Fatherhood

There is one area of this prayer that I do not try to explain in full detail. It is the question of why Jesus

refers to God only as *abba*, "Father." Although I do
clarify Jesus' use of the term *Father*, a full explana-
tion of this notion would take us too far from the
book's theme — *Setting a Trap for God*. Jesus was
not sexist nor antifeminist. For further study on the
biblical representation of God as Father within its
cultural context, I recommend Professor John W.
Miller's book *Biblical Faith and Fathering: Why We
Call God "Father."*[1]

Scriptural Quotations

Most of the biblical passages and excerpts are my
translations from the Aramaic Peshitta text, both Old
and New Testaments.[2] I do not identify my translations; the attribution is accomplished generally by
the use of a listing following the quote. This listing
will be enclosed in parentheses and will consist of
the book, chapter, and verse from which I am translating. (In a few instances, the attribution appears in
a slightly different format: instead of parentheses,
a long dash is used to introduce the attribution.)
However, I have also taken a few quotes from *Holy
Bible From the Ancient Eastern Text* by George M.
Lamsa, Th.D., and each quotation is identified as the
"Lamsa Translation." There are also a few quotes
appearing in this book from the King James Version
of the Bible, and the abbreviation "KJV" follows
each of these citations.

---

1. See the bibliography for more details on the book.

2. See the bibliography for the Aramaic text and manuscript.

A Final Word

My sincere desire is that you may find inspiration and guidance in this book. May your spiritual affinity and sensitivity increase and bring blessings into your life with great abundance. May your union with the living Presence we call God be always renewing and constantly fortifying itself.

—Rocco Errico
April 1996

Chapter One
Setting a Trap for God

Modern terms such as *affirmation*, *visualization*, *mind treatment*, *active imagining*, *treasure mapping*, and *master minding* make the use of the word *prayer* definitely appear outdated. Everyone seems to have special ideas about what it means to be in contact with universal, spiritual forces. There are many individuals who think that prayer is simply *telling God (spiritual forces) what to do*. Others imagine that God, omnipresent Mind, or the boundless universe is like some huge, magnificent *Cosmic Vending Machine* cranking out cars, homes, money, health, relationships, and whatever other notion may pop into the mind.

In ages long past, hoary Semitic savants and language makers gave birth to a unique Semitic word *slotha* that we have translated in English as *prayer*. This word *prayer* in its original sense from the ancient Aramaic tongue has a distinct meaning. And we can better understand the intent of this Semitic term by uncovering its root significance and relevance.

It is very difficult, when translating from one language to another, to retain the authentic impact and power of a certain word or thought. We usually lose something through translation. The task is even more challenging when it involves such vastly different cultures as our Western culture and that of the Near or Middle East. For example, this has been and still is a problem in translating the Bible from Eastern Semitic tongues (Aramaic and Hebrew) into Western languages.

The Aramaic Language

Aramaic was the Semitic *lingua franca* (universal tongue) of the ancient Near East. It made its historical appearance toward the end of the second millennium BCE. Aramaic began making inroads throughout Near Eastern lands and was the language of the Arameans, Assyrians, Chaldeans, Hebrews, and Syrians. It was also the language of the Persian (Iranian) government in its western provinces. This language is still spoken today in many areas of the world.

Aramaic and Hebrew are sister languages. Many of the root words for the Hebrew tongue are Aramaic roots. The native tongue of Jesus of Nazareth was Aramaic. He spoke, taught, and proclaimed his joyful message (gospel) all over Palestine in his own language.[1] His famous "Our Father" prayer (which we also call the Lord's Prayer), was composed in Aramaic.

The Aramaic Meaning of *Prayer*

The word for *prayer* in Aramaic is *slotha*. It comes from the root word *sla*, which literally means "to trap" or "to set a trap." Thus, *prayer* in its initial sense implies "setting your mind like a trap so that you may catch the thoughts of God"—in other words, "to trap the inner guidance and impulses that come from your inner spiritual source."

1. See Rocco A. Errico, *Let There Be Light: The Seven Keys*, Noohra Foundation, Santa Fe, 1994, pp. xxviii–xxx and pp. 2-4.

6

Prayer also means "a state of mind in which we still all personal thoughts and make no attempt to project anything outwardly." It is an "alert state of total sensitivity and attentiveness."

Other Meanings of *Prayer*

In Aramaic the word *slotha* carries other meanings such as these: "to focus," "to adjust," "to incline," and "to tune in." A modern way to say it would be "to select a channel." If I were going to speak to you in Aramaic and ask you to turn on the television set to a particular channel, I would have to use the Aramaic root word *sla* for prayer. And it would mean "to select the proper channel," "to adjust the set," or "to tune in the desired program."

Setting the Trap

In prayer, then, we are *adjusting* and *preparing* our *minds* and *hearts* to *receive God's program*. God (spiritual forces) is always broadcasting and televising. The heavenly and universal transmitter operates around the clock and never goes off the air. Spirit is constantly beaming, sending, and signaling to everyone and everything in creation. Infinite, loving Intelligence is everywhere and through everything.

"Setting a trap for God" is the ancient meaning of prayer. And, it suggests that we can trap all the love, joy, truth, peace, energy, and compassion we need when we are receptive to all which is rightly ours. It is truly an attitude of heart and mind that prepares us for whatever is necessary. This kind of prayer qualifies us to receive God's provision and, in turn, to express gratitude and thankfulness.

A Modern Illustration

There is an illustration I like to use when explaining the ancient meaning of prayer. It is like owning a videocassette recorder. There are two ways we can make use of it. We can use a videotape on which a program has already been recorded or we can use a blank one. Usually we use a blank tape to record a program that is coming on the invisible air channels to our set. Undoubtedly, it is helpful if our tape is clean so that it can receive the clearest recording possible.

Genuine prayer prepares the mind to become a blank tape ready to receive all the good that we may need in our lives. When our minds are free, open, clear, and sensitive, we can trap the power and presence of God. For God counsels not with words but by Spirit—the intangible.

The awareness of God's presence is what brings health and power in our hearts, lives, families, relationships, and financial needs. Universal powers and forces are never against us. Spiritual forces that reside within us and flow through us are always present. They are guiding, aiding, and supplying—if we are trapping and working with the universal program and not just our own agendas.

The Meaning of *God*

Now that we understand *prayer* as "setting a trap for God," what do we mean by the term *God?* People hold different views about God. Some picture God as a kind, but stately old man with a long, white beard, dressed in dazzling, luminous robes. They also visualize him seated on a gold throne and having a place we might call "central headquarters." Interestingly, this depiction of God derives from the Canaanite god whose name was *el.* *God* as a word simply means a "deity." The Aramaic term for *God* is *alaha.* In Arabic it is *allah,* and in Hebrew *elohim* or *alohim.* All these words for *God* derive from the same Semitic root—*al* or *el.* There are various ideas about the Semitic root meaning of this word. Here are a few examples: (1) the strong or mighty one, (2) the revered one, (3) the highest one (Canaanite root), and (4) the helper, the supporter, the one who sustains (Aramaic root).

Another Aramaic term for *God* is *ithea,* "self-existent," "self-cohesive and sustaining." This term is qualitative and refers to the eternal existence, i.e., something that exists of itself and does not derive its life *from* anywhere or *through* anything else. In other words, God is all there is. Everything we call a "thing" derives its existence from *ithea.*

The self-existent principle known as *ithea* in Aramaic is the efficacious, creative Presence. This Presence permeates and acts throughout the universe. It effectively keeps evolving our awareness of its power and maturing our individuality. *Ithea* flows in us and out from us always.[2] It has its own sustaining energy. *Ithea* is the force within and behind the universe that keeps everything on the move. This universal Power is the same living, sustaining Presence that abides within us.

2. For a further comprehensive search into the meaning of *God,* see Rocco A. Errico, *The Mysteries of Creation: The Genesis Story,* Noohra Foundation, Santa Fe, 1993, pp. 46-59.

The Consciousness of a Near Easterner

If one were to ask a spiritually devout Easterner what *God (alaha)* means to him, he would not reply in theological terms or creeds. His answer would be put in simple, direct language: "*Alaha* is my *very breath*, my *very heartbeat*, and my *life*." For the Semitic consciousness, the living God encompasses and watches over him as a skilled shepherd unceasingly watches over his flock.

The words of the poetic psalmist describe this awareness very clearly. He sings of his devotion and thirst for the living God. He knows that wherever he may be, the reality of God's nearness is always there. An Easterner knows that God is aware of his very thoughts and conduct. He declares that it is too wonderful to fully understand:

> As the hart pants after the waterbrook
> so pants my being after you,
> O *Yahweh!*[3]
> Thirsting for you is my very being
> O living God!
> When shall I come to see your face? . . .
> Deep cries out to deep
> at the sound of your waterfalls.
> —Psalm 42:1-2, 7

---

3. The Aramaic text uses *mariyah*—"LORD." However, I employed the Hebrew text here in my translation. It uses *YHWH* which usually translates as *Yahweh*, the name of Israel's God. Some scholars suggest that the Aramaic term *mariyah* derives from two Aramaic words: *mar*—"lord" and the abbreviated form of the name *Yahweh*—"*yah*." Thus, in Aramaic the term *Mariyah* may have originally meant "Lord Yah."

O Yahweh,
You have thoroughly examined me and known me.
You know how I conduct my life.[4]
You have discerned my thoughts from on high.
You know my way and my paths,
You have closely followed all my ways.
If there is any change in my speech,
O Yahweh,
You know it completely,
from the first to the very last.
You have formed me
and placed your hand upon me.
For me, such knowledge is too wonderful!
It is powerful!
I cannot master such power!

Where shall I go from Your spirit?
Or, to where shall I flee from Your presence?
If I ascend into the heavens,
You are there.
If I descend into Sheol,[5]
Behold, You are there also!
If I lift up my wings like those of an eagle,
and dwell in the far-out parts of the sea,
Even there shall your hand lead me,
and your right hand shall hold me.
—Psalm 139:1-10

4. Literally it reads: "You know my sitting down and my rising up." This is a Semitic idiom and refers to one's conduct and behavior.

5. *Sheol* is a common Hebrew word that refers to the "abode of the dead." It occurs 65 times in the Bible.

Infinite Intelligence Is Everywhere

Since *alaha*, *God*, is everywhere present and is the essence of all life, we can easily see that we are living in an eternal, spiritual universe. This living Presence fills the cosmos. The entire cosmic system is vital and dynamic. There is order in it all! There is intelligence in it all!

Let us take, for example, the tiny seed. It is a living chemical factory endowed with an intelligence all its own. The seed knows how to trap solar energy and convert it into itself. Today, we humans are attempting to learn this special secret. The seed also knows how to work with the law of death. It knows how to disintegrate itself, to shed the old outer hull, and to release its new life. This seed, then, gives the world food to help sustain life; it helps beautify our planet and make it a habitable place.

It is through our intelligence that we commune with the living God. This intelligence within us is highly intuitive and sensitive. We understand and *feel* our union with God (spiritual forces) intuitively and *not just intellectually.*

Inner intelligence governs the physical body and regulates all living cells that make life and health. "It is the Spirit that gives life" (Jn. 6:63). In other words, the spiritual intelligence within us grows our physical forms. Our bodies are in the constant care of God or Infinite Intelligence. This awesome power continually and spontaneously works to heal all psychic and physical wounds.

Let us recall the idea that God fills the entire universe, for God is Spirit, and *spirit* means "that which is everywhere present." Therefore, the counsel and guidance we may need is ever present for us to tap. But, it often happens that we do not stay in tune to receive the guidance we need. Through negative mental attitudes, we tune into *other* channels, such as fear, worry, jealousy, and resentment. And sometimes we turn our *receivers* off completely!

So, we must consciously and actively *tune in* to God's guidance and counsel. After all, God is both *around* and *within* us, as Scripture clearly says: "For *in Him (God)* we live and move and have our being" (Acts 17:28). The apostle Paul also says, "To whom God wanted to make known the riches of this   glorious mystery among the nations; which is the Messiah-Christ, the expectation of our glory" (Col. 1:27).

We can learn to move *with* God through the power of prayer. The Lord's Prayer teaches us good and wholesome attitudes that are required for a state of communion with our own inner spiritual forces. Through prayer we learn to "tune in" to all the good there is. We are not tuning into anything peculiar or foreign. The only way it could possibly appear to be strange or peculiar is if we have not become aware of our spiritual natures.

Spiritual powers have always been within the hearts and souls of all human beings. But we often look for something that is outside of ourselves, not fully realizing that we are God's image and likeness. Just as the entire universe and its elements have their own functioning powers, so we, too, have our own capabilities that we can utilize. These powers are inherent because we are humans. We can participate with God.

A Misconception of Prayer

Prayer is not "telling God" what to do. God knows how to run the universe! We do not need to remind God of our needs nor of the needs of our relatives and friends. "And when you are praying, be not babbling like the pagans, for they are expecting that through the abundance of words they will be heard. Thus, do not be like them, for your *Father knows what you need*, before you ask Him" (Mt. 6:7-8). So, prayer is not "telling God," but it is listening to what God would tell us.

The purpose of prayer is *not to change God*, but *to change us*! Do we really think that through prayer we can move God to do something God would not otherwise do? No prayer can make God more loving than God already is, or was in the past or shall be in the future.

What prayer accomplishes is this: It helps us to understand ourselves. It attunes us to spiritual forces around and in us, and it nourishes our spirits. Prayer brings a clearer atmosphere into our minds so that we may better comprehend our world and other human beings.

We must also fully realize that we can *consciously* work with this inner intelligence to guide us in solving the problems we face in life. This is the reason Jesus gave us his form of prayer. I refer to his style of prayer as *attuning attitudes*. There is only one Power in the universe, and through the goodness of this one Power, we can face our fears and overcome them.

Our fears generally create blockages that hinder us from knowing the inner guidance we need. It takes courage, truthfulness, and freedom to face ourselves squarely. In other words, we must have courage to see our fears, hates, and resentments. But, by so doing, we shall most naturally and spontaneously tune out inappropriate attitudes and tune in to the good around us. Our minds and hearts are then, at that moment, free from fear, which limits and restricts the creative intelligence within us. Our fear closes the door to practical and sound living, but freedom opens the door of life for our good.

Jesus' understanding of prayer was one of direct and intimate communion with life forces—*alaha*. God is the essence of all life, both visible and invisible, tangible and intangible. Prayer is our means of hearing the quiet and gentle voice of the loving presence we call God.

When we attune our minds with the proper attitude, we can trap the counsel of God. When we do this we become "of one accord" with spiritual forces. "I and my Father are one." Or, I may translate it as, "I and my Father are in agreement" (Jn. 10:30). This idea enables us to live in harmony with God's universal principles instead of opposing them. In other words, these principles can guide us in everything.

Praying in Jesus' Name
We have often heard evangelists and preachers admonishing us to pray "in Jesus' name." This

command comes directly from the Gospel of John as a saying of Jesus to his disciples:

> In that day you will not ask me for a thing. Truly, truly, I say to you that anything you may ask my father in my name he will give it to you. Until now you have not asked for a thing in my name, ask and you will receive, so that your joy may be complete.
>
> —John 16:23-24

Just what is the secret of praying in Jesus' name? Is it merely uttering the name *Jesus* after each prayer or petition? We need to realize that the name *Jesus* was a common one in Palestine during his lifetime. With so many men bearing the name *Jesus*, there could be nothing special in the utterance of that particular name. Then what did Jesus mean when he asked his disciples to pray in his name?

To truly pray "in his name" means "to pray with the same kind of understanding about God and the human family that Jesus had." The Aramaic term *beshemi*, "in my name," implies "according to my way, method, approach, technique," or "with my kind of understanding." Jesus encouraged his disciples to pray to the Father in his name, but he meant for them *to pray in the manner he taught them.*

For example, scientists have learned the secret of splitting atoms through Einstein's method or formula. However, scientists do not command the atom and say, "In the name of Einstein, Atom, split!" And yet, many well-meaning people use Jesus' name in this way and expect something special to happen. It is as if there were magic in uttering the name. Merely saying his name will not cause the desired results any more than saying the name of Einstein will make the atom split of its own accord.

The answer to praying in Jesus' name, then, lies in *knowing and experiencing* the same awareness that Jesus had and felt:

- That God is a *loving parent;*
- That God is *the source of all good;*
- That God is *for us* and never against us;
- That we are His children;
- That as His children we can *receive* all *good things* a loving parent has for us.

This is the spiritual equation that Jesus revealed and taught. Living in this awareness positively negates all that is not good.

Practicing Jesus' Teachings

Jesus took a small group of simple young men from Galilee and taught them the secrets of prayer and God's kingdom. Through these young men, Jesus changed the course of the world. He showed them what it meant to be a child of God. He endowed them with spiritual insights and gifts to help all humanity in transforming this world. His teachings empowered his disciples so that they could overcome the problems created by a limited consciousness.

We, too, can learn to apply his teachings in our lives and thereby live a more fruitful and abundant life. There is nothing complicated or difficult about

Jesus' method. His teaching is simple, but we sometimes stumble at simplicity.

Jesus taught his disciples a new way of praying because he knew certain things they did not know. He knew that human beings do not have to beg and beseech God to give them the good things of life, as if God would not otherwise have done it. In prayer we need to understand that all good in the universe is always present for us. God has given everything that we as humans may need for our well being. Jesus also knew that our capacity to receive good is limited only by a restricted realization to claim and accept it.

Again, Jesus said, "And if, then, you who make mistakes know how to give proper gifts to your children, how much more shall your Father who is in heaven give beneficial things to those who ask Him" (Mt. 7:11). We human beings make mistakes. Yet, we still know how to give proper gifts to children. Since this is so, then, how much more does God know how and when to bestow beneficial things.

Jesus opened the door for everyone to the kingdom of heaven when he told us that the kingdom is "within you" or "among you." The pronoun "you" is plural. "When some of the Pharisees asked Jesus when the kingdom of God would come, he answered and said to them, 'The kingdom of God does not come through much watchfulness. And they will not say, "Behold, here it is!" or, "Behold, it is there!" For lo, the kingdom of God is within you (in your midst)' " (Lk. 17:20-21).

This means that the kingdom is within our reach, but we must act to lay hold of it. The Pharisees were

students and teachers of the law. They examined
Scripture with great scrutiny and carefully watched
for the kingdom of God to come. They did not realize the important role that every individual plays in
the manifestation of God's kingdom.

Quality vs. Quantity

According to Jesus the Spirit of a human
being and God's Spirit are of the same essence.
He understood the divine revelation that declared
human- kind the "very image and likeness of God"
(Gen. 1:26-27). This essence is the same in "quality"
but, of course, not the same in "quantity." For example, a little spark of fire is of the same essence or
"quality" as a great flame or a raging inferno, though
not of the same "quantity."

God and humans, then, being of the same spiritual
essence, are able to commune—*the infinite with the
Infinite*. It is wonderful to realize that all humans
have the power to capture God's ideas and guidance.
This equips us with all we need to solve our problems and to mature spiritually.

Unity with God makes our thoughts creative. Our
creativity enables us to continually be coworkers with
the natural spiritual energies that flow to us, in us,
and out from us. And it is by *tuning in* to Spirit that
we learn to create that which is good and wholesome.

It is from this spiritual world of unseen realities that all discoveries and creative ideas come. All
things visible have come from the realm of the invisible. Our minds are part of that invisible, spiritual
world. Thus, we can trap, interpret, and direct many

hidden realities into our physical world of matter so that we may all benefit.

Enlightenment and all good gifts come from above, that is, from *our Father*. The apostle Jacob (James) tells us: "Every good and appropriate gift is from above, and comes from the Father of lights, in Him there is no variance nor shadow of change" (Jas. 1:17). It is through prayer that we discover the Source of all good gifts which come from above.

A Traditional Short Prayer

Some biblical authorities tell us that the Lord's Prayer was not totally original with Jesus. They claim that portions of this prayer were prayed in the synagogues during his time. They also say that Jesus placed a different emphasis on various parts of this synagogue prayer and rearranged the focus.

However, other modern scholars of the New Testament tell us that half the prayer did not originate with Jesus at all. They think and teach that his prayer first went something like this:

Our[6] Father
Holy be thy name
Come Your kingdom
Give us our needful bread from day to day
And forgive us our offenses even as
we have forgiven our offenders
And do not let us enter into temptation[7]

6. Certain NT scholars believe that the prepositional pronoun "our" was not a part of the original prayer of Jesus. They hold to the idea that "our" in Matthew's gospel is typical Matthean style. They claim that Jesus only used *abba*, "Father."

7. This line of the prayer also has come under the scrutiny of NT authorities, and they find it questionable. Some think Jesus did not compose this phrase of his prayer.

For an opposite view, Professor Irving M. Zeitlin says that "Jesus composes and recites a direct, simple, succinct prayer that is truly remarkable for the universality of its appeal and the brevity with which it conveys its earnestness and devotion." Again, Professor Zeitlin tells us:

> It has long been recognized among students of first-century Judaism that there are many affinities between the language of the Lord's Prayer and that of both the Hebrew Scriptures and rabbinic prayer. Some scholars have painstakingly demonstrated that every word and phrase of Jesus' prayer can be traced to biblical and rabbinic sources.... "Our Father who art in heaven" is an expression found in many Jewish prayers.... The phrase, "Thy will be done, as in heaven, so on earth," appears in the "short prayer" of the early *Tanna*[8].... The expression "Give us this day our daily bread" is found in a similar form not only in the Hebrew Scriptures ... (Prov. 30:8), but in a variant of Rav Eliezer's "short prayer."[9]

Joseph Klausner, a brilliant Jewish scholar, also remarks that the Lord's Prayer "can be divided up into separate elements, every one of which is Hebraic in form and occurs in either the Old Testament or the Talmud." Nonetheless, he clearly sees

8. *Tanna*: The rabbinic authorities of the first two centuries, from Hillel and Shammai to Rav Yehuda ha-nasi.

9. Irving M. Zeitlin, *Jesus and the Judaism of His Time*, Polity Press, in association with Basil Blackwell, Oxford, 1988, p. 111.

and contends that Jesus did form something fresh and unique:

> Jesus gathered together and, so to speak, condensed and concentrated ethical teachings in such a fashion as to make them more prominent than in the Talmudic *Haggadah* and the *Midrashim*, where they are interspersed among more commonplace discussions and worthless matter ....
>
> Although there is in the Mishnah, an entire tractate devoted exclusively to ethical teaching, viz., *Pirke Aboth* [the Ethics of our Fathers], it is but a compilation draw-ing on the sayings of many scores of *Tan- naim* ...; *but the ethical teachings of the Gospel, on the contrary, came from one man only and are, every one, stamped with the same peculiar hallmark. A man like Jesus, for whom the ethical ideal was everything, was something hitherto unheard of in the Judaism of the day.*[10]

In conclusion, one more idea needs mentioning. We turn again to Professor Zeitlin who declares his belief in Jesus' unique religious creativeness:

> There is, then, no denying Jesus' originality. For it should be underscored that although portions of the Lord's Prayer have parallels in other Jewish prayers, taken as a whole, it is a unique entity. The Lord's

---

10. Joseph Klausner, *Jesus of Nazareth*, Macmillan, New York, 1943, pp. 387-9, italics added, tr. Herbert Danby.

Prayer may therefore be considered Jesus' original creation: an extraordinarily beautiful, private prayer of the truly devout.[11]

As for the matter of whether Jesus composed the entire prayer, half the prayer, or that a particular gospel writer added his ideas to the prayer makes no difference for me. Why is this so? Because it is the power, light, and Truth of the prayer that counts. The entire prayer is consistent with the spiritual tenor of the time.

Tolstoy and Jesus

Leo Tolstoy in his religious and spiritual search for the meaning of life and its purpose came to this realization. He declared:

The chief matter ... is not whether Jesus was God, or from whom descended the Holy Ghost, or when and by whom was a certain Gospel written, or *if it may not be attributed to Christ*; but the light itself is of importance to me, that it still shines upon me after eighteen hundred years with undimmed brightness; *but how to call it, or of what it consists, who gave it existence*,[12] is immaterial to me.[13]

Regardless, Jesus created this short prayer through his own creative spiritual genius and drew upon the inspiration that flowed through the depth of his being. He gave prayer a vital and pragmatic synthesis.

11. Zeitlin, Blackwell, p. 112.

12. The italics (for emphasis) in this quote are mine.

13. Leo Tolstoy, *The Spirit of Christ's Teachings*, Walter Scott, London, p. 161.

23

A Mini-Gospel

The Lord's Prayer contains *the essence of Jesus' entire teachings.* It is a capsule summary of the message he declared throughout Palestine. It contains the message of the Torah and the prophets. Even if we were to lose access to Scripture but retained the Lord's Prayer, we would still have the essence and meaning of religion.

Genuine Religion

Spiritual awareness is innate and is an essential part of our beings. We must have order and balance in our lives. And this is exactly what *religion* means in the Aramaic language. *Dina*, "religion," in Aramaic means "balance"—a balance in our own beings and an equitable, balanced relationship with others.

Jesus' prayer, then, is a brief summary of his beliefs about God, humanity, and the world. This prayer is a synopsis of his understanding of the relationship between the material realm (the seen) and the spiritual realm (the unseen).

Teach Us to Pray

Jesus' method of prayer is a simple and direct *acceptance* of the good the universe has for us. He knew that God, like a caring, providing parent, is interested in the welfare and the well-being of His human family.

There is really no great secret about communing with the innate spiritual forces that reside in us. But it will help us if we understand Jesus' idea of spiritual forces (God) and thus let go of ideas that are stumbling blocks and hindrances to us.

The Lord's Prayer: A Translation

When Jesus' young disciples were with him one day by the Lake of Galilee, they asked him to teach them to pray. Jesus immediately began to instruct them in his way of prayer. He told them to pray "this way." The short phrase "this way" means to pray "something like this":

> Our Father who is everywhere,
> Let Your name be set apart.
> Come Your kingdom (counsel).
> Let Your desire be, as in the universe,
> also on the earth.
> Provide us our needful bread from day to day.
> And free us from our offenses, as also we have
> freed our offenders.
> And do not let us enter into temptation,
> but separate us from error.
> For belongs to You the kingdom, the power,
> and the song and praise,
> From all ages throughout all ages.
> (Sealed in trust, truth, and faithfulness.)
> —Matthew 6:9-13[14]

14. A literal translation from the Aramaic *Peshitta* text by the author.

Chapter Two
Abba—Father

In Matthew's gospel we find Jesus opening his prayer with the words *awoon dwashmaya:* "Our Father who [is] in heaven." I may also translate the phrase as: "Our Father who [is] throughout the universe," "Our Father who [is] everywhere," or more freely translated, "Our universal or heavenly Father." Jesus comes right to the point. He instructs his disciples to approach God as Father directly, without intermediaries.

Calling God "Father" during that time was not entirely unusual but Jesus did place a special emphasis on the expression "Father" especially in his prayer. He perceived and stressed the closeness of God not as a vengeful deity but as a compassionate parent. Jesus envisioned God's awesome and mighty presence being approached in a childlike way, by calling this Presence *abba.*

The immense contrast between the notion of an awesome deity and the appellation *abba* must have been startling for his disciples and the people of his day. In our modern world we think of God as Supreme Being and Creator. We use Latin-derived terms such as omnipresent, omniscient, omnipotent, and omniactive to describe the majestic power of God. However, Jesus' approach was completely unpretentious and uncomplicated! His reality of God was much simpler—"Dad." This contrast of calling the Almighty "Dad" is overwhelming even for us.

Bernard Brandon Scott, associate professor of New Testament Studies, St. Meinard School of Theology, says the following in regard to the Aramaic term *abba*:

> In Aramaic *Abba* is the child's word for father, equivalent to the English "daddy." As an invocation it burlesques formal invocations, an irreverence that Matthew's tradition remedies with the proper liturgical invocation, "Our Father who art in heaven." *Abba*'s poking fun at formalism has been overlooked in the past, but such language is typical of Jesus. Just as Mustard Plant burlesques Great Tree, so *Abba* burlesques a formal, solemn approach to God. The invocation is a shock to the everyday way of prayer....
>
> But precisely because *Abba* imaginatively conjures up childhood feelings of intimacy and dependency, for those who so address God the immense distance between God and themselves has collapsed. That is, they see Reality as Whole, not as Divided. Eschatology is realized; for them the Kingdom has come. Furthermore, the use of the child's *Abba* destroys the Status of God's formal title, indicating that *Abba* is a title of Grace.[1]

1. Bernard Brandon Scott, *Jesus, Symbol-Maker for the Kingdom*, Fortress Press, Philadelphia, 1981, p. 150.

Jesus clearly stresses God as a parent and nothing more. We miss the purpose of this prayer if we become caught up with the idea of masculinity versus femininity. He is not accenting the maleness of God[2] but accentuates the parental presence of God.

We also know that in first-century Judaism, most sincere Jewish believers were inclined to place God farther and farther from the living world of humanity. Apocalyptic thoughts concerning the coming of the Messiah, God's wrath, and drastic impending judgments were influencing the Palestinian population.

Jesus, like those who embraced apocalyptic thought, was deeply interested in the oppressed. But, his approach to God and the oppressed was totally distinct from apocalyptic thinkers. God was not a wrathful, unapproachable deity but a caring, guiding, providing parent, a father.

Jesus knew God as a father who loved all His children, even those who had gone astray. Calling God "Father" created the idea of an intimate, loving, and compassionate Presence. He taught direct, one-on-one communion with God as "Father."

James H. Charlesworth, professor of New Testament language and literature at Princeton Theological Seminary, also gives us more insight into Jesus' use of the Aramaic term *abba*, "Father":

Yet, Jesus chose to use *'abbā'* not *'abinu* when addressing God, and he put a unique emphasis on the word *Abba*. It was his

---

2. In the Hebrew Bible, *Yahweh*, the God of Israel, appears to be a male deity.

habitual way of referring to and calling God. Is it not conceivable that he called God *"Abba"* because he had a conception of God that was in some ways different from that of *most* of his contemporaries? Many early Jews *tended* to conceive of God as distant, visiting humanity only through intermediaries such as angels, as we know from studying the Pseudepigrapha and the Dead Sea Scrolls. Jesus perceived that God himself was very near, and that he was directly concerned about each person, even (perhaps especially) sinners.[3]

Before this time, when the people prayed, they didn't pray just to God. The petitioners' cries would be, "O, Father Abraham; O, Father Isaac; O, Father Jacob." Abraham, Isaac, and Jacob became intermediaries. It was as if, for their forefathers' sake, but not their own, God would possibly hear them and grant their petitions.

But Jesus made known to them, through his prayer, that God was their Father and that God was concerned for them. God was aware of all their needs. They did not need to approach God through the Hebrew patriarchs. They didn't need *any* mediators. People could have *direct communication* with the Father, for they, too, were just as important as their ancestors!

Almost immediately we can see the lesson for us.

3. James H. Charlesworth, *Jesus Within Judaism: New Light From Exciting Archaeological Discoveries*, Doubleday, New York, 1988, p. 134. Professor Charlesworth is also chairperson of the department of biblical studies at Princeton Theological Seminary.

We need no mediators or "go-betweens" when communing with God. *No one* in the past, in the present, or in the future has to be sought so that we may commune with our Father. According to Jesus' teachings, we don't need any priest, rabbi, minister, or guru to approach God. *We are our own priests and our own intermediaries!* Jesus revealed each person's individual relationship with God.

God Is an Approachable Parent

In this remarkably simple prayer, Jesus nowhere mentions the word *God*. He uses the Aramaic term *abba,* "Father," or, as it appears in the text, *awoon,* "our Father." This gives us a sense of nearness. It is almost like saying "daddy" or "papa." Jesus taught his disciples that God is like a good father who is benevolent and kind.

As I mentioned earlier, at that time, God was depicted as some mysterious, awesome, and fearsome deity who lived far from His creations. God was so far removed from them that even His precious name was too holy for them to utter. Others believed God was coming with swift judgment to punish wicked people and nations. But Jesus laid all that aside, for he taught his disciples that when they approached God, their attitude should be that God was "Father."

In other words, "our heavenly parent" is approachable. We can always come to God. But how can we come near to a deity who is too far above us, too great, and too holy and full of anger?

God dwells in such awesomeness, who can draw near? "You cannot see my face; for no one can see me and live!" (Ex. 33:20) We quake and tremble with fear at such revelation.

Again, Jesus changed this idea of God. He knew God's true nature. The Creator is not a presence that we must fear. To the contrary, God is a presence with whom anyone can commune.

Jesus told his people that God was like a good father who would lead, guide, and protect them. God wants good for everyone, and we can come to God without shame and doubt. We need not waver or hesitate.

Sonship Now

Many Bible instructors continue to teach that we must approach God as if we were totally degraded, full of sin, no good, and unworthy human beings. This is not interpreting Scripture correctly! Jesus *never* taught this! There were many people to whom Jesus declared his gospel who were not degenerates or sinful, depraved souls. For example, he acknowledged the good and kind qualities people possessed when he gave the Beatitudes. Read Matthew 5:1-12, and note how he spoke to and taught the crowds.

He *didn't say,* "Blessed are those who are *going to become* merciful," or "who are *going to become pure* in their hearts," or "who are *going to become* peacemakers." (Not that he would exclude anyone who *might become* merciful, pure in his/her heart, or a peacemaker. This is not the point.) Matthew records Jesus as saying: "Blessed *are the merciful*"; "Blessed *are those who are pure in their hearts*"; and "Blessed *are the peacemakers.*"

Certainly, there are those who *are* merciful, who *are* pure in heart, and who *are* peacemakers. Jesus drew out the good in people. Naturally, there were those who were going astray and were losing their way on the path of life. But Jesus also taught the means for them to find restoration and reconciliation. No matter how far one might stray, there was and always is the opportunity for renewal and rejuvenation. Repentance,[4] which means "turning to God," and forgiveness were Jesus' methods for restoration. (See Lk. 24:46-47.)

Approaching God as a "parent" immediately puts us in intimate communion with this loving Presence. Prayer is not an attempt to *become one* with God or to *get in* union with God. Prayer is the very expression and recognition of our oneness and union with God!

It is because we *are* His children that we can talk with our Father. *At no time* can there be a split or *separation* from this Presence! If we believe that we are cut off or separated from the parental presence of God, then it is we who bring this sense of loss and division. God does not do this; it is our own mental attitude or thought that divides us. God *is*! And God is everywhere! *God* does not change! *We* need to change our mistaken ideas and beliefs of separation from God!

When we call God "Father" we acknowledge our sonship with Him. We don't *work* our way into

4. The word for *repentance* in Aramaic and Hebrew refers to the action of *turning* or *returning*. According to widely attested Jewish sources: "Returning to God, His covenant, and the practice of good works brings salvation." See Rocco A. Errico, *The Message of Matthew: An Annotated Parallel Aramaic-English Gospel of Matthew*, Noohra Foundation, Santa Fe, 1991, p. A-9.

33

sonship; we naturally have it because we are "His image and likeness." With the opening phrase of the Lord's Prayer we confess our union with the eternal, living God, the "Father" of all humanity. This is the theme we must maintain throughout the entire prayer — God as our loving parent!

Thus, the first idea we gain and the prime attitude we *tune in* to, is that we are one with our heavenly parent now! All creation is in union with Infinite Intelligence. Once we genuinely accept the Truth of our sonship, we do not have to affirm it! We need to come to the full realization that *we are now* God's children, and we have always been His children! "My beloved ones, now are we sons (children) of God, and yet it has not been revealed what we shall be. We know that when he shall be revealed, we will be in his likeness because we are seeing him as the being he is" (1 Jn. 3:2).

Universal Presence

We often misuse and misunderstand terms such as *condescend* and *transcend* concerning the relationship between God and humanity. "Our Father" doesn't *condescend* to hear us or to be with us, because, like a loving human parent, He enjoys being with His family. God does not have to *condescend*, nor do we have to *transcend*, to be in union with this living Presence. Of course, we can transcend our environment and problems, but what I refer to is our relationship with spiritual forces. God is Spirit, that is, that which is all-inclusive and everywhere. How can God *come down*, or how can we *go up?* God is *in* us, *above* us, *around* us, *underneath* us, and *through* us! Jesus made this very clear to the Samaritan woman at Jacob's well:

> Jesus said to her, "Woman, believe me, there will be a time when neither on this mountain nor in Jerusalem will you worship the Father. You worship something you do not understand but we worship what we know because life is from the Jews. But the time will come, and now is, when true worshipers will worship the Father in spirit and in truth because the Father wants worshipers such as these! Because God is spirit and those who worship him must worship him in spirit and in truth [that is, with understanding]."
>
> —John 4:21-24

It is not just a "Deity" that is everywhere; it is a powerful parental spirit that is everywhere. This Presence is like a caring father giving good gifts, love, and aid to His children everywhere. The parental presence of God is in the very depths of our beings.

God can't be confined to any sacred shrine or contained in any one thing. No holy temple can house the universal Spirit of the living God. Even King Solomon, after he had built the great and magnificent temple in Jerusalem, prayed on its opening and dedication day: "Behold, heaven and the heaven of heavens cannot contain you, how much less this house which I have built?" (1 Kings 8:27)

The great prophet Isaiah knew that Yahweh (the Lord God) was more than just a God to the Hebrews. Isaiah knew that the God of Israel was the God of the universe and that no one could confine God to any shrine or temple. This is what Isaiah tells us:

> Thus says *Yahweh*, Heaven is my throne and the earth my footstool; what is this place that you build for me? And where is the place of my rest? For all those things has my own hand made, and all those things belong to me, says *Yahweh*. And to whom shall I look, and where shall I dwell? Only to him who is calm and humble, and trembles at my word."
>
> —Isaiah 66:1-2

All Races Are Children of God

"Our universal Father" also means that God is the Father of all peoples and all races. The Creator is not just "my" Father, or just "your" Father, but God is "our Father." When we say the words "*our* Father who is everywhere" we immediately recognize other peoples' sonship with the parental presence of God. It is God's Spirit that fills the universe, and all things as well as all people exist through this Presence. This means that the Chinese, the Russians, the Japanese, the Arabs, and all races everywhere are sons (children) of God!

God loves *all* His children! But when we pray, we frequently pray *only* for our *own good*, not caring about its effect on others. For instance, in warfare, we often ask and beseech God to bless one side or the other. God cannot bless either side, for God does not participate in acts of violence or aggression. The parental presence of God acts only for the good of *all!* When we truly and deeply understand the meaning of "our Father who is everywhere," we *will* pray for not only our good but for *universal* good. We *will* empathize with *all* nations and *act* for the good of *all*.

The Meaning of *Heaven*

The phrase *dwashmaya* literally means "who [is] in heaven." I placed brackets around the verb "is" because in the Aramaic text this verb is not present. Before concluding this chapter with the first attunement, we are going to examine the word *heaven* a little more closely to help us understand the phrase "who is in heaven."

Shmaya is the Aramaic word for "heaven" or "heavens." In Hebrew it is *shamayim* — "heavens." This Semitic term can also mean "sky," "universe," "cosmos," and, by implication, "everywhere." The idea of heaven among ancient Near Eastern religions is very interesting.

According to early Mesopotamian legends, heaven emerged as a deity spreading its splendor everywhere. However, the Egyptian storytellers in their myths inform us that when heaven separated from earth, the gods climbed up to heaven and made it their abode. Heaven was populated with all classes of gods and goddesses. Various activities took place in the heavens. These Near Eastern gods and goddesses held court and made very important decisions as well as great judgments.

To the contrary, the Hebrew creation account (the first chapter of Genesis) plainly proclaims heaven as a creation of God and nothing more. Heaven is the place for the winds, snow, clouds, and hail. The winged creatures are to fly in its great expanse. (See Job 37:9; 38:22; Ps. 135:7; Jer. 10:13.) The celestial bodies occupy the heavens. The sun, moon, and stars are the genuine celestial dwellers. Clearly, the biblical author does not work with a mythical idea of heaven. According to the author of the Genesis account, it is not God's abode. Heaven is not a domicile for any divinity or personage.

Then, from where do we obtain the idea that God is in heaven? This idea comes directly from other passages of Scripture and not from the Genesis creation account. The poets, prophets, songwriters (psalmists), and other Israelite authors tell us the heavens were the habitations of God.

These biblical sages used ancient tales and traditions to express their poetic, figurative, and descriptive language about God and His dwelling. They tell us God is enthroned in heaven and meets with His heavenly court, He rides the clouds as one would ride a chariot, earth becomes His footstool, and He fills the heavens with His mercy and compassion. All these sayings and a multitude of similar ones are Semitic figures of speech.[5]

In a final note, Israelite authors also used the term "heaven" as a metaphor. They employed it to signify peace and harmony. In Chapter 5, "Will—

---

5. For more history on "the firmament" and "heaven," see Rocco A. Errico, *The Mysteries of Creation: The Genesis Story,* Noohra Foundation, Santa Fe, 1994, pp. 100-103.

Wish—Desire," I explain more about the meaning of heaven.

The First Attunement

Jesus, through his teaching, freed us from the limiting and mistaken notion of a sectarian, nationalistic, partisan God. Spirit, or "God," is like pure water which flows freely everywhere, watering the dry ground and quenching the thirst of all. We must have water and air to live. Clean water and pure air are the same everywhere. And so is the parental presence of God. This is Jesus' idea of the living God, whom he called *abba*, "Father," and whom he taught us to recognize as "our Father."

Thus we proclaim and confess, through the opening line of the Lord's Prayer, our union with God and with our fellow humans who are all children of God. This is God's way! This is "our Father who is everywhere"! What an affirmative and beneficial way to begin prayer! We have begun setting the trap. This is our first attunement.

Chapter Three
Set Apart

Nithqadash shmakh means "Holy be Your name." One may also translate the phrase as "Let Your name be set apart (set aside)." The word *qadeesha* means "pure," "holy," "a holy one," or "saint." It comes from the Semitic root verb *qdsh,* "to be holy," "to hallow," "to sanctify," "to consecrate," "to set apart for a specific purpose," "to dedicate for a holy use or to a cause," "vowed to God," "to be distinct," or "to separate for an honorable function."

For example, if I said to you, "Please *set* that drinking cup *aside* for the lecturer this evening," then that particular cup becomes *holy.* In other words, the cup is *set aside* for a specific function. No one would use that special cup for any other purpose except the lecturer that evening.

During Jesus' time and, no doubt, even before his time, people were using God's name *falsely.* Jesus reminded his disciples and followers to keep God's name holy, that is, apart from abusive deeds and unjust transactions. God's name represents all that is good and wholesome. His name means that God is "distinct" and has the set purpose of enlightening the human family in all the ways of good and well-being.

False Oaths

In the Near East, when merchants sold articles, they would call upon God's name during their bargaining. These men usually would raise a hand to heaven and swear in God's name, taking an oath something like this: "In the most precious name of God *(alaha)* and all His holy angels (messengers), this shirt is worth $20, but you, my dear friend, may have it for a special price of only $14." One's reply might be, "In the most glorious names of the saints (Blessed be God!), this shirt is not worth $8, but I'll give you $10." Often bargaining would last for an hour or two, using not only the precious names of God, but all the names of specific angels, saints, and even special members of the merchant's household. All the glorious names that the heavens above contained might be spoken.

The Near-Eastern salesman would speak all the beloved names to bolster the sales pitch. And if the retailer should fail to sell his article, he might become angry, swear, and possibly expectorate. This use of God's name in everyday business was unnecessary, according to Jesus. The sellers dragged God's name down into lying oaths and misleading conversations.

Jesus was against the use of God's name in false oaths, as we can see in his comment recorded in the message of Matthew: "But let your words be, 'Yes, yes,' or 'no, no'; anything more than these is from a deceiver" (Mt. 5:37). In other words, if one should call on God's name in an oath, then that individual needs to speak the plain, straight, truth! Better for the conversation to be simply, "yes, yes", or "no, no." But, even to this very day the practice of using the Creator's name in everyday business still continues. And undoubtedly many individuals, not just in the Near East, use God's name in false and deceptive ways.

The Third Commandment

Jesus' authority for this teaching was one of the Ten Commandments that Moses received while communing with God on Mt. Sinai (See Ex. 19:16-25 and Ex. 20:1-17). It is the third commandment to which Jesus refers. The usual rendering of the third commandment is, "Thou shalt not take the name of the Lord [Yahweh] thy God *in vain* [emphasis added]." (Ex. 20:7 KJV). This phrase "in vain" is not an appropiate translation.

The Aramaic word is *dagalootha,* "in falsehood." Thus, a more appropriate translation would be: "You shall not take the name of the Lord (Yahweh) your God in falsehood." God's name is to be kept apart from *lying* words and *false* oaths.

Other Fallacious Applications

Religious people have used and still use God's name harmfully and wrongfully in many other ways. In His name, they have carried on *holy wars,* persecutions, crusades, ethnic cleansings, and massacres. Masses, in the name of God and in their fanatical zeal, have killed innocent men, women, and children thinking that they were doing God a great favor. It was and frequently still is believed that it is a divine virtue to murder those of an opposing or differing religion, belief, and faith. This is not only confined to religious teachings, but also to varying political views and divergent lifestyles.

False prophets and fraudulent teachers have taught destructive and erroneous doctrines in God's name, backing them with holy Scripture. They do this to suit their own desires and exalt their private beliefs. These prophets and teachers, through their misleading teachings, have darkened many souls and have clouded the minds of countless people, inciting them to take harmful actions.

The Holiness of God

God is holy. He is apart from all error and evil. But His holiness doesn't mean that God is unapproachable, distant, or aloof. Many have a mistaken idea about God's holiness. God is dedicated to the good of all humanity, for, after all, He created us in "his image and likeness."

"But like the Holy One who has called you, *set yourselves apart* (be holy) in your entire manner of living. Because it is written, 'You shall sanctify yourselves and be holy, for I am holy.' "[1] The idea of *holiness* means to be "distinct," in Hebrew, *perushim tiheyu*. For the people of Israel, this meant that they, in becoming a holy nation, must keep themselves distinct from other nations. They were to be a model so that other nations could see what it would be like to have spiritual forces directing a people in all matters social and political. In the Jewish book called the Sifra,[2] the idea of holiness as "otherness" is explained.

1.   1 Peter 1:15–16. The reference to the Hebrew Bible is Leviticus 11:44 and 19:2.

2.   Sifra—*Torat Kohanim*. A tannaitic midrashic commentary to the Book of Leviticus, probably compiled at the end of the 4th century C.E.

The idea of God's holiness reminds us that He takes no part in evil transactions or in deeds that hurt, destroy, or kill people. This is why Jesus told his disciples to pray, "Hallowed (holy) be thy name." Let us realize that "our Father's" name is holy—separate from error and falsehood—for God has no part in untruth. God manifests Himself in all glory and goodness.

God's Holy Name

We must always keep in mind that in this prayer, one is addressing *abba*, Father. Therefore we are speaking of the holiness of "Father" and not just a deity's holiness. This is what makes the prayer so unique and so like Jesus. Again Professor Scott tells us:

> The setting apart of his name will invoke a healing wherein all will be drawn into the intimacy of *Abba*. At first glance, the petition to hallow or set apart appears to understand Reality as Divided, which would be unique in Jesus' language. But the name to be set apart is *Abba*, which connotes Reality as Whole, Status as destroyed. This transforms "hallow" so that the setting apart of such a name encompasses all within it— Reality becomes divisionless as it returns to its childhood, to when God is *Abba*.[3]

We must always keep in mind that the prayer is directed to *abba*—Father. Whether the prayer speaks

3. Scott, pp. 150-151.

of the name, will, power, or glory, it is always connected to the Father.

The Second Attunement

God's name represents all that is good and wholesome. So let us speak God's name in goodness and Truth only. We recognize and acknowledge that all good surrounds the name of God as "Father." We know that God as a father is for the good of all humanity. The parental presence of God and the holiness of His name is for our good also. All good surrounds us in His name. This is our second attunement.

Chapter Four
Heavenly Counsel

Taythey malkuthakh means "Let your kingdom come." Jesus, in his heart and mind, had transcended racial, religious, and nationalistic boundaries! He foresaw a world in which God's rule as a parental presence reigned in the hearts and souls of men, women, and children everywhere.

However, most of his people were looking for an earthly, partisan kingdom. They were eagerly yearning for and expecting the long-overdue restoration of the Davidic kingdom. They wanted the Romans defeated, Herod dethroned, and the rule of Israel established again. The prayers of the people were constantly directed to this end and for this type of kingdom.

The dreams, visions, and hopes of apocalyptic authors and believers in the God of Israel were seeing the end of their present age. They also believed that God's wrath was coming and could foresee the collapse of their present world order. They longed for God's leadership to take action and conquer the then-current gentile rulers so that Israel would be restored to its former glory.

The Spiritual-Social Kingdom

Jesus' vision was not apocalyptic. He shifted the emphasis away from the usual manner of praying for God's coming as king. He taught his disciples to pray for God's kingdom and not for the Davidic (political) kingdom. The prayer is for a genuinely spiritual, social kingdom—a reality that rules from inside the hearts and minds of all human beings—a kingdom where God rules or counsels. Of course, this heavenly leadership would eventually affect and change the politics of the land.

However, this kingdom was not a political, materialistic kingdom that would be imposed upon human- ity from without. He knew that human rule *alone* without God's leadership as Father would bring strife and division. Jesus knew that God's king-dom embraces all nations and peoples impartially. In God's rule, authentic justice prevails for all, because one equal measure is extended to all nations and peo-ples. Because of God's rule as *abba*, Father, all politi-cal structures would be affected. All races and nations are His children. Now, let us examine the Aramaic word for kingdom from a linguistic point of view.

Counsel and Advice

Malkutha, "kingdom," derives from the root verb *mlkh* (or *malkh*) and means "to counsel," "to advise." It is the same root for the words *king, advisor*, and *counselor*. Thus, God's kingdom from a Semitic and semantic point of view also denotes God's sovereign counsel. Linguistically, the kingdom of God is a state in which God's guidance as a Father is carried out.

In this kingdom, the *Inner Being* rules, not with force and regulations, but with celestial, parental counsel and loving-kindness. When we pray this phrase of the Lord's Prayer, "Let your kingdom come," we are actually saying, "Let divine, spiritual forces (Father's wise counsel or parental loving advice) guide our lives and direct us in all our ways." Since this spiritual guidance is parental in its nature, we are totally dependent on *abba*—as little children would be dependent on their parents.

Jesus explicitly tells us that we need to become like little children to enter the kingdom of God. "In that very hour the disciples approached Jesus asking: 'Who is the greatest in the kingdom of heaven?' So Jesus called to a little boy and made him stand in their midst, and he said, 'Truthfully I tell you, unless you change and become *like little children,* you shall not participate in the sovereign counsel of heaven' " (Mt. 18:1-3).

Again, Jesus told his disciples, "Permit the little children to come to me and do not hold them back; because the sovereign counsel of heaven is *for such as these*" (Mt. 19:14). One can see from Jesus' sayings that we need to change our attitudes and become as little children to enter God's kingdom. Jesus looked at reality from a different perspective. He perceived it from his inner experience with God's presence, that is, from *abba*'s presence, from Father's sovereign counsel.

God's Kingdom

God's counsel will always guide us away from trouble, when we consult the Father within and heed spiritual direction. Our difficulties needlessly multiply because we usually do not seek God's kingdom—counsel. In reality, we inwardly know the truth of God's guidance, but we don't act on it.

The kingdom of God is universal and upholds justice and equality for the entire human family. But we usually look only one way. That is, we look out just for ourselves. We typically pray only for *our* nation and for *our* way of life.

Yet, when we sincerely pray "Let your kingdom come," we petition God's counsel to reveal itself to us so we may carry it out in our lives. Father's counsel is just and balanced. It's not a long measure for this person and a short measure for another. The measure is the same for all. When God's leadership comes, it is fair and just. It is extremely difficult for human beings to be totally just when counseling; it is commonly one-sided. Someone is going to be short-changed somewhere. But God's kingdom, that is, God's sovereign counsel, is always fair for all concerned.

The Kingdom Present or Future?

Jesus was a Galilean, Aramaic-speaking teacher and prophet. He was a Shemite, a spiritual, religious genius. He went throughout Galilee declaring the joyful message of God's kingdom (sovereign counsel).[1] Mark, in his gospel, apprises us of the situation. "Jesus came to Galilee, proclaiming the joyful message of God's sovereign counsel (kingdom), saying, 'Time has come to an end, God's sovereign counsel is present! Turn (return) to God and have confidence in this joyful message' " (Mk. 1:14-15).

---

1. One may also translate "God's kingdom" as "God's sovereignty." This is in keeping with the Semitic meaning of the word *kingdom*.

There is absolutely no uncertainty that Jesus proclaimed the joyful message of the ever-present counsel of God. New Testament translators usually render the expression *malkutha dalaha* as "kingdom of God" or, as "God's imperial rule." I prefer to render it as "God's sovereign counsel." It is the recognition and actualization of God's counsel through every one of us that manifests the kingdom here and now.

The Greek word for kingdom is *Basileia*. It also means a "realm," "region," "kingly power, authority, dominion, reign, or imperial rule." However, as I mentioned above, "kingdom" in Aramaic is *malkutha* and in Hebrew, *malkuth*. "Realm or territory" is not the Semitic meaning behind the word *malkutha*. It is God's "sovereignty," not God's "territory." Simply put, the kingdom represents God's presence.

"King" in Aramaic is *malka* and in Hebrew, *melekh*. This term "king" was originally "counselor"—he whose view and idea is decisive. Thus, God's so-called "imperial rule" is not a political realm that will impose itself upon humanity. Recall that all these words come from the Semitic root *mlkh* or *malkh* meaning "to counsel or advise."

God's reign, which is subtle in its administration, is in reality His sovereign counsel. It is difficult for us to recognize God's kingdom as being present or being among us. Jesus had told his disciples and followers that God's kingdom was "at hand," but its coming, that is, its recognition, was not so discernible.

The Unobservable Kingdom

"And when the Pharisees asked Jesus when God's sovereign counsel was coming, he replied and said to them, 'The sovereign counsel of God cannot be recognized by sight. No one will be able to say, "Look, here it is!" Or, "Look, it is there!" It is just the opposite; God's sovereign counsel is present among you!' " (Lk. 17:20-21).

Jesus understood that God governed through His divine counsel and that it was present everywhere but not so easily discerned. He presented many parables that acknowledged God's powerful sovereignty as working now in people's hearts, minds, and souls. (See the parables of the kingdom in Matthew's gospel, Mt. 13:1-53.) According to the four canonical gospels, there is also the idea of the final coming of God's kingdom, that is, when it is universally recognized and actualized.

God's counsel is always here for us. When we are ready to open ourselves to our innate spiritual strengths, we come to realize heaven in our lives and on earth. But, we may ask, how does God counsel?

What we call "God" is the powerful spiritual presence of love, compassion, peace, joy, and abundant supply. God does not literally give advice as one person would advise another. The manifestation of God's kingdom on earth can only come about through the human family. As we open ourselves to the latent harmonious forces in and around us, we soon discover we are not helpless creatures lost in a maze of confusion.

Clarity and understanding spring up within us

like a living well of water as our souls unite with our own spiritual energies. These spiritual powers are not only self-healing, but they are also directed towards others. Conflicts may never cease, but they can be healed peacefully through God's counsel.

The movement of God's kingdom is God's omni-active healing presence in and through the lives of men and women all over the world. Only the dynamic and vigorous energy of spiritual powers flowing into and out from the heart of humanity can bring heaven to all the nations. No political power in the past, present, or future has been or will be able to fully assure joy, peace, freedom, and harmony for humankind. Laws and legislation alone cannot rule the human heart or heal the world's ills.

So-called apocalyptic judgments, that is, wars, famines, and catastrophic upheavals, have not brought and *cannot* bring global peace. John the Baptist warned his people that the wrath of God was coming and that the Messiah was soon to appear. He was full of apocalyptic expectation. But when he was arrested and no political changes occurred, he doubted that Jesus of Nazareth was the one he and others like him had anticipated.

John, while in prison, sent messengers to Jesus and asked him:

> Are you the one who is to come, or are we to expect another? Jesus replied and said, "Go and tell John the things you see and hear—the blind see, the lame walk, lepers are cleansed, the deaf hear, the dead

raised, and the poor are given hope. Delighted is he who does not stumble on my account."

—Matthew 11:3-6

The point is that physical, mental, emotional, and spiritual healings being active for everyone are the signs and indications of God's kingdom on earth. These things evidence God's active rule and presence. For Jesus said, "And if by God's spirit I am healing the insane, then God's sovereign counsel has come to you" (Mt. 12:28). Again, apocalyptic judgments (wars, earthquakes, and calamitous events) are not the signs of the kingdom or the end of the present age. "And this joyful assurance of the kingdom shall be proclaimed throughout the world for a testimony to all nations; and then the end shall come" (Mt. 24:14). Jesus' kingdom message was one of power, healing, forgiveness, reconciliation, and love for God and humanity.

He did not condemn those who had lost their way. He healed broken hearts, physical and mental illnesses, and wrongs people had committed against themselves and others. God's power and kingdom were confirmed through diverse spiritual events and healings. Hate, fear, and resentment are mental and emotional forces that can only find cleansing and release in the pure and clear healing stream of God's counsel. The kingdom, ever present, is always functioning and working for us.

Kingdom as Symbol

The kingdom is really a symbol that points to a

greater Reality—a reality which is not totally comprehensible but is apprehensible. We must intuit the presence of the kingdom, for it is the presence of God. It takes the nonrational mind to fully grasp the symbol of the kingdom. Reason alone cannot take hold of the symbol—God's kingdom. This is why it is here and yet is in the future. Again, we may ask, why do we pray "Let your kingdom come" if it is here? Once more, Professor Scott explains it this way:

> The prayer calls for the Kingdom's present experience to be consummated by granting to others the experience of its coming. Since the coming involves the appearance of Reality, it also involves its contrary Illusion.... Reality's final coming means that those living under the Illusion that the Kingdom has not been established will realize that in Reality it has come....
>
> The petition requests both that others may experience the coming of the Kingdom and that the Kingdom come—that all may experience God as *Abba*; that Reality may dispel the Illusion surrounding it; that the Kingdom of God break out of its boundary.[2]

Paul in his letter to the Romans says this about the kingdom: "Now, God's sovereign counsel is not food and drink, but goodness,[3] peace and joy in the

2. Scott, pp. 151-152.

3. Piety.

Holy Spirit" (Rom. 14:17). And again, he tells us: "The kingdom of God is not in word but in power (*haila*—'energy')" (1 Cor. 4:20). We enter a new reality when we enter God's kingdom, that is, when we let God rule in our lives.

God's Kingdom First

"But first you search for the sovereign counsel of God and his justice and all these things shall abundantly be given to you" (Mt. 6:33). To "search for God's kingdom first" means to open our minds and hearts to God's guidance, above all else. When we do this, then all of our needs, material and otherwise, flow to us and out from us.

God's direction will always lead us into paths of blessing. It will enable us to solve our challenges, both individually and nationally, as we clearly perceive it and act upon it. When we positively act on divine guidance, we need not feel any anxiety about *our way,* for we are seeking the best way for all, and *all* includes us too. Fear torments us, but faith and confidence in God's kingdom bring peace and satisfaction.

The Third Attunement

Let us turn to and act upon God's ever-present kingdom (counsel). Let us also take the necessary steps to look beyond just our own interests and see a larger world of peace and harmony for all races and nations. When we pray in this manner, our prayers and thoughts become universal. We earnestly feel and want good made manifest for all.

Undoubtedly, we do many things that are good, and we maintain many attitudes that are wholesome. This is God's presence now moving through us. "For it is God who inspires you with the will to do the good things which you desire to do."[4]

Let us open ourselves fully to God's counsel and live our lives within its wisdom. It is then that we live a life which *naturally* yields peace and harmony. The kingdom's power and guidance begin *within*! It is our choice! This is our third attunement.

4. Philippians 2:13, Aramaic Peshitta text, Lamsa translation.

Chapter Five
Will—Wish—Desire

The Aramaic words *nehweh seweeyanakh akanna dwashmaya ap barah* mean "Let your will be, as in heaven so on earth." Literally the words translate as "Let your wish (desire) be, as throughout the universe, also on earth." The Semitic word *seweeanah* is very important for us to understand. It means "will," "wish," "desire," "delight," and "pleasure."

The Will of God

Frequently we think of the "will" of God as something mystifying, elusive, unpleasant, or sanctimonious. And, worst of all, people often feel that *God's* so-called will is contrary to *their* will. We also equate the word *will* with the word *willful* or something that is being *forced* upon us.

When we understand "the will of God" as a father's *good desire* or *pleasure* for his children, its meaning becomes clearer. For instance, Luke's gospel reports Jesus as saying, "Don't be afraid little flock because your Father *desires* (*wills* or *wishes*) to give you the kingdom" (Lk. 12:32). The Aramaic verb *swa* means "to will," "to wish," "to desire," "to be willing," "to delight," "to please," or "to pleasure." It is also the root of the noun *seweeanah*— "will." Now we can see that in the Lord's Prayer, the word *seweeanah* ("will") does not imply that God is going to impose something distasteful upon us.

No Cause for Dismay

What, then, is the will of God? I have frequently been asked this question. And many times in my years as a pastor have I counseled individuals who were struggling "to know the will of God" for their lives. There were so many who felt the burdening pressure of guilt because they thought they were not doing "God's will." People suffer such frustration trying to discover the will of God! What is meant by the term *will* in this phrase of the Lord's Prayer?

Let us return for a moment to Jesus' original thought. In the opening phrase, Jesus said *awoon,* "our Father," or *abba,* "Father." He did not pray to *God Almighty.* It is clear that the prayer refers to a parent's caring and loving will or desire. It does not refer to the will of some awesome, terrifying Deity! This is something that God as Father wishes for us and does not demand of us.

What kind of loving parent would God be if He made it difficult for us to learn or to know His will? And if God did, in reality, have a "will" for us, then He would want us to *know* His divine will.

What Is God's Wish or Desire?

Let us keep in mind that this is not our concept of "God Almighty" with whom we are communing, but it is *abba,* "Father"—a loving, spiritual, parental Presence that abides within us. What does a parent wish or desire for his or her children? Let me ask you, What do you wish for your children? What do I wish for my children? What would our "will" be for our children or anyone's children?

I think the first thing we would desire for our children is that they be healthy. Next, we would wish that they be happy, prosperous, and able to get along with others; that they may have peace of mind; that they may understand others and relate well with them; that they may find peace and harmony, not only among themselves as brothers and sisters, but also in their many other relationships. Finally, we would wish that they may have the wisdom and maturity to journey safely on this planet and stay out of trouble.

Is not all of the above what we would desire for our children? We want good things to happen for them. Is this not our "will" for our children? Since this is true for us, why then do we complicate the matter of God's will?

Jesus said it so warmly and clearly when he spoke to the men and women who were standing around him: "And if, then, you who make mistakes know how to give proper gifts to your children, how much more shall your Father who is in heaven give beneficial things to those who ask him?" (Mt. 7:11)

Since we know how to give good gifts to our children, although we make mistakes, how much more then must our heavenly Father, who never makes mistakes, know how to provide good for us. It is God, as Father, who has bestowed intelligence upon us to care and provide for our children. So then, our heavenly Father's "will" is for us to have health, prosperity, understanding, peace, and harmony within ourselves and with others. This is "the will of

God" for us! This is God's desire for us!

We don't have to beg our Father to find out what His will is! He is a parent. He wants us to live freely and happily. It is just that simple! Truth is never complicated nor is it difficult. Thus God's will is not enigmatic or perplexing to understand. Jesus changed the whole religious idea. God's will is a caring parent's will or wish.

God Does Not Inflict Suffering

How many times have we heard that it is the "will of God" for us to suffer? And, when we are sick, we may even question our *right* to become well. Or we may believe that God wants us to be sick so that God may teach us compassion and empathy for others. But this is not God's way of teaching us compassion and empathy. We bring this on ourselves.

Is it not because we have improperly understood our "Father's will," that we may have resigned ourselves to a life of poverty, illness, loneliness, and suffering? Then, there is the so-called religious belief that suffering and poverty is godly. This, also, is a false notion.

When our children become sick, don't we do everything in our power to make them well? Loving and caring parents would not inflict suffering on their children to teach them a lesson. We want our children to learn and to be sensitive and empathetic, but we do not want them to become ill so that they may learn some lesson about life.

If we who make mistakes know how to give good and appropriate gifts to our children, how much more so does our heavenly Father! No, our Father does not send us sickness to teach us a lesson. We bring misfortune on our own heads without the help of God. Hopefully though, when our suffering hurts badly enough, we will wake up to the error of our ways of thinking and change the habits that brought on our troubles.

God does not inflict evil upon people! Diseases, for example, manifest themselves when we break natural health laws and principles. Sometimes we become insensitive to our bodily needs. Then again, we may be violating the laws of a healthy mind. When this happens, hatred, resentment, and bitterness may manifest themselves in our bodies as various forms of illnesses.

Our environment both within and without can also create sickness as well as certain unhealthy cultural patterns. I say these things merely to reveal that it is not God who brings these physical challenges and disorders. Usually we create these problems by going against our own good, either through ignorance or deliberately having to have our own way in a particular matter.

Disease does not originate with God. And it is healthy for us to recognize that God is always *for* us. And when God is *for* us, who or what can be against us? The apostle Paul tells us: "What then shall we say about these things? Since *God is for us,* who can be against us?" (Rom. 8:31) He further informs us, "And we know that those who love God are helped *by Him in everything for good.*"[1]

1. Romans 8:28, Aramaic Peshitta text, Lamsa translation. The italics are not in the text. I put them in for emphasis.

Universal Harmony

Shmaya means "sky," "heaven" or "heavens," "cosmos," and "the universe." Metaphorically, it refers to "peace," "harmony," and "prosperity." Ancient savants and prophets used the term "heaven" to indicate a "universal state of peace and harmony."

Heaven also refers to a personal consciousness of peace and harmony. These prophets and wise men used the idea of the "heavens" because they had observed how the planets and other celestial bodies stayed in their orbits. Our own observations tell us how harmoniously the astral bodies function.

Through the centuries, humankind has gradually learned why this is so. Today, we also know that there are natural and unchangeable laws built into the elements of the physical universe that create these planetary systems and make them perform in definite and harmonious ways. By merely being just what they are, the elements of the universe express these inner laws. And they naturally function together in a balanced manner and in complete accord with each other. The essence of the universe is order and intelligence. Now we can understand why the ancient teachers used the heavens as a metaphor to express harmony and balance. The prayer says, "Let heaven's harmony manifest itself on earth among humankind."

Religion Is Balance

Our English word *religion* comes directly from the Latin language, and it is spelled the same — *religion*. The Latin root is *religare* (*re* — "re" and *ligare*—"to tie or bind"), "to retie" or "rebind." In Aramaic there are two words used for religion; one is *dina* and refers to "balance." The other word is *urha* and means "the way" or "path." Just as each planet or star in the universe is dependent on other heavenly bodies, so we, too, are interdependent and interrelated with one another. If we remove the cohesive balance and order from within the universe, we will have chaos. The same thing happens in our communities when there is no order, balance, or intelligence functioning in our society. Chaos and violence will dominate everything.

The intelligence we call "God" is that very cohesive power and energy which keeps everything in order and balance. Religion is the study of order and balance that results from the operation of divine laws. Spiritual laws of the soul keep society working together. When a society loses its soul as a whole, then we have chaos. Thus, religion teaches us to keep a just, balanced relationship within ourselves, with one another, and within our environment.

Do You Likewise

Jesus gives us an example of how God's will (desire) is to be carried out on the earth, exactly as it is carried out in the heavens. That is, we need to be cooperating with, instead of working against, the internal laws of our being. These spiritual laws are God-given inclinations to do good.

Jesus teaches us that we are to be sensitive to the spiritual principles and energies which are within us if we would have peace. Just as the elements of the universe move in harmony with their innate laws, so we, too, need to flow with our innate spiritual powers. In this way, we will live together in peace and harmony.

The natural laws of the universe are designed for flawless operation. But when we decide to interfere and break the laws of our beings, we move out of our own orbit. And what happens when we move out of orbit? We collide and harm one another, and everyone suffers. But by understanding ourselves, and by working with the laws that govern our souls and existence, we can avoid collisions and much unnecessary pain, anguish, and distress.

The Fourth Attunement

By understanding and working with each line of the Lord's Prayer, not only does setting the trap become powerful, but we also tune in to our eternal Source. The prayer aligns us with the harmony that prevails throughout the universe. When we say these words in sincerity, we admit that we desire God's wish *to be on earth* just as faithfully as it is in the heavens. By awakening this attitude within ourselves, we open our consciousness to the possibility of universal peace on earth. We prepare ourselves to receive and acknowledge the good that our loving Father constantly gives to us.

The more we enter the realization and efficacy of the prayer, the more the power and spiritual forces flow through us. As we pray these words, we confess that we want to stay in our own orbits. We allow the genuine inner Self to emerge and not collide with others. We affirm with all our hearts that we will work with our intrinsic powers and strengths. These inner forces allow us to express the same beauty, harmony, and oneness that we see being expressed throughout the universe. Let them flow out among those with whom you associate. As we attune ourselves to our Source, we communicate these divine forces that are within us to others. We feel and radiate truth and life to all. This is the fourth attunement.

Chapter Six
Matthew 6:9-13 — Aramaic Text

The Western Aramaic Peshitta Text —
The Lord's Prayer

אֲבוּן דְּבַשְׁמַיָא.

נֶתְקַדַּשׁ שְׁמָךְ.

תֵּאתֵא מַלְכּוּתָךְ.

נֶהְוֵא צֶבְיָנָךְ

אַיְכַּנָא דְּבַשְׁמַיָא: אַף בְּאַרְעָא.

הַב לַן לַחְמָא דְּסוּנְקָנַן יַוֹמָנָא.

וַשְׁבוּק לַן חַוֹבַּיְן:

אַיְכַּנָא דְּאַף חְנַן שְׁבַקַן לְחַיָּבַיְן.

וְלָא תַעְלַן לְנֶסְיוּנָא.

אֶלָּא פַּצָּן מֶן בִּישָׁא.

מֶטֻּל דְּדִילָךְ הִי מַלְכּוּתָא.

וְחַיְלָא וְתֶשְׁבּוּחְתָּא.

לְעָלַם עָלְמִין.

אַמֵין

The English Translation of the Western Aramaic Peshitta Text of Matthew 6:9-13— The Lord's Prayer

Our Father who is everywhere,

Holy be Your name.

Let Your kingdom (counsel) come.

Let Your will (desire) be

as in the universe, even so on the earth.

Provide us our needful bread from day to day.

And forgive us our offenses,

even as we have forgiven our offenders.

And do not let us enter into temptation

but free us from error.

Because Yours are the kingdom,

and the power, and the glory

from all ages, throughout all the ages.

Amen.

The Eastern Aramaic Peshitta Text of Matthew 6:9-13 —The Lord's Prayer

ܐܒܘܢ ܕܒܫܡܝܐ.

ܢܬܩܕܫ ܫܡܟ.

ܬܐܬܐ ܡܠܟܘܬܟ.

ܢܗܘܐ ܨܒܝܢܟ.

ܐܝܟܢܐ ܕܒܫܡܝܐ: ܐܦ ܒܐܪܥܐ.

ܗܒ ܠܢ ܠܚܡܐ ܕܣܘܢܩܢܢ ܝܘܡܢܐ.

ܘܫܒܘܩ ܠܢ ܚܘܒܝܢ:

ܐܝܟܢܐ ܕܐܦ ܚܢܢ ܫܒܩܢ ܠܚܝܒܝܢ.

ܘܠܐ ܬܥܠܢ ܠܢܣܝܘܢܐ:

ܐܠܐ ܦܨܢ ܡܢ ܒܝܫܐ.

ܡܛܠ ܕܕܝܠܟ ܗܝ ܡܠܟܘܬܐ

ܘܚܝܠܐ ܘܬܫܒܘܚܬܐ:

ܠܥܠܡ ܥܠܡܝܢ

ܐܡܝܢ.

The English Translation—Each Word

Our Father

who [is] everywhere (heavens),

Holy be

Your name.

Let come

Your kingdom (counsel).

Let be

Your will (desire or wish)

even as

in [the] heavens (universe),

also

on [the] earth.

Give us (Provide)

bread

for our needs

The Pronunciation of Each Aramaic Word

awoon   ܐܒܘܢ

dwashmaya   ܕܒܫܡܝܐ

nithqadash   ܢܬܩܕܫ

shmakh   ܫܡܟ

tethey   ܬܐܬܐ

malkuthakh   ܡܠܟܘܬܟ

nehweh   ܢܗܘܐ

seweeyanakh   ܨܒܝܢܟ

akana   ܐܝܟܢܐ

dwashmaya   ܕܒܫܡܝܐ

ap   ܐܦ

barah   ܒܐܪܥܐ

haw-lan   ܗܒ ܠܢ

lahma   ܠܚܡܐ

dsunqanan   ܕܣܘܢܩܢܢ

from day to day.

And forgive us

our offenses,

even

as

we

have forgiven

our offenders.

And do not

let us enter

into temptation

but

free us

from evil (error).

Because

Yours is [are]

[the] kingdom,

and [the] power,

yaumana	ܢܘܡܢܐ
washwok-lan	ܘܫܘܩ ܠܢ
haubain	ܚܘܒܝܢ
akana	ܐܝܟܢܐ
dap	ܕܐܦ
hnan	ܚܢܢ
shwakan	ܫܒܩܢ
l'hayawen	ܠܚܝܒܝܢ
wla	ܘܠܐ
taalan	ܬܥܠܢ
l'nisyona	ܠܢܣܝܘܢܐ
ella (ela)	ܐܠܐ
pasan	ܦܨܢ
min-bisha	ܡܢ ܒܝܫܐ
mitol	ܡܛܠ
ddeelakhee	ܕܕܝܠܟ ܗܝ
malkutha	ܡܠܟܘܬܐ
whaila	ܘܚܝܠܐ

and [the] glory

from all ages,

throughout all ages.

Amen.

wtishbohta   ܘܬܸܫܒܿܘܚܬܵܐ

la-alam   ܠܥܵܠܲܡ

almeen   ܥܵܠܡܝܼܢ

Amen   ܐܵܡܝܼܢ

Chapter Seven
Bread From Day to Day

The Aramaic phrase *hawlan lahma dsunkanan yaumana* means "Provide us our needful bread from day to day." Before we begin explaining the meaning of *bread* in this prayer, let's take a look at the attitude of Eastern people toward bread. In the Near East, people live more simply than we do here in the West. They are content with the provision that comes each day.

For example, Eastern women do not make up a supply of bread to last for several days. Instead, they bake their bread every day for that day alone. And not only do they bake enough for their own family's needs, but they also bake extra bread for the needs of travelers and strangers who might happen to stop by seeking food for their journey.

Easterners are hospitable to travelers whenever they stop, be it day or night. They believe that the stranger they share food with today may be their own host tomorrow. Therefore, they treat each other well and even share with their enemies.

To this very day certain desert bedouins will treat even their greatest enemies with profound courtesy. They will serve them food and protect them with sword and shelter. This protection and housing will last for three days only—especially if they made a "bread and salt covenant." (However, if the so-called enemy understands Near-Eastern etiquette and has any intelligence at all, he will flee for his life before the sun sets on the third day.)

Consecrated Bread

Near Eastern Semites believe in the sacredness of bread. For instance, an Easterner will often say, "There is bread and salt between us," meaning, "we are one by a sincere, solemn agreement." The phrase "bread and salt" is a venerable one. If anyone breaks the covenant of "bread and salt," people consider him base and unworthy of trust. The saying about this offender of the "bread and salt" covenant will be, "He knows not the meaning of bread and salt." This is a stigma that holds forever.

Normally an Easterner will not tell a lie while bread is present on the table. They believe that bread has a mystical sacredness because it is God's provision for one of humankind's basic needs. Where else could daily bread come from but the caring, providing, loving hand of God for all humanity. The late Dr. Abraham M. Rihbany from Lebanon tells us:

> As the son of a Syrian family I was brought up to think of bread as possessing a mystic sacred significance. I never would step on a piece of bread fallen in the road, but would pick it up, press it to my lips for reverence, and place it in a wall or on some other place where it would not be trodden upon.

What always seemed to me to be one of the noblest traditions of my people was their reverence for the *'aish* (bread; literally, "the life-giver"). While breaking bread together we would not rise to salute an arriving guest, whatever his social rank. Whether spoken or not, our excuse for not rising and engaging in the cordial Oriental [Near Eastern] salutation before the meal was ended, was our reverence for the food (*hir-metel-'aish*). We could, however, and always did, invite the newcomer most urgently to partake of the repast....

The *'aish* was something more than mere matter. Inasmuch as it sustained life, it was God's own life made tangible for his child, man, to feed upon. The Most High himself fed our hunger. Does not the Psalmist say, "Thou openest thine hand, and satisfieth the desire of every living thing"?[1]

Daily Bread

A Semite's entire life centers on God. Everything he or she does is done in God's most precious name. In God's name the head of the household plants his seed in the freshly plowed ground. He repeats God's name when he is ready to harvest his crop and spreads his sheaves on the threshing floor. When he grinds his grain at the mill, he does it all calling on the blessed name of God.

1. Abraham M. Rihbany, *The Syrian Christ*, Houghton Mifflin Co., Boston, 1916, pp. 193-95.

Eastern women also knead their dough and bake bread in the name of God. When they serve their families with their bread, it is with the sense of God's continual blessing upon them and their provisions. Therefore, the expression is given in the Lord's Prayer: "Provide (Give) us this day our daily bread." It is a constant reminder that it is God who provides them with bread.

For them there is a feeling of deep gratitude to the Giver of all good and perfect gifts. It is almost impossible to explain the emotional and spiritual attitude Easterners have toward bread. Daily bread is also a reminder of God's presence that is ever with us providing whatever is necessary. A Semitic poet put it this way:

"Back of the loaf is the snowy flour,
Back of the flour the mill;
Back of the mill is the wheat and the shower
And the sun and the Father's will."[2]

Eastern Bread

When you visualize Eastern bread, do not picture a "loaf" of bread, as we have today. The bread of the Eastern people is similar to a Mexican tortilla—very thin, flat, and round. You can hold a tortilla in your hand, but Eastern bread is very large, about 10 to 12 inches in diameter. It is possible to feed thirty to forty people on one loaf of Eastern "bedouin" bread. Once, when I was on my way to Damascus, I shared a loaf of this bread with approximately forty people who were traveling with me.

2. Ibid., p. 197.

This loaf of bread can be folded like a handkerchief and carried in a pocket. In ancient times this is what people did when they journeyed in the Near East. Inns were scarce; therefore, Easterners had to carry their food with them for the entire trip.

It was also their custom, when they sat down to eat, to offer their food to anyone else present. Thus, when they were journeying and walking along the road, some would secretly pull food out of the hidden places in their robes. They did this so that others could not see them eating. In this way, they were not obliged to offer their limited and dwindling supply of bread. Proverbs 9:17 refers to this ancient custom when it says, "Bread eaten in secret is pleasant." However, this proverb also has another connotation—a hidden double meaning.[3]

Various Meanings of *Bread*

Bread not only means the actual bread itself but also "food." Symbolically it represents "ideas" and "prosperity." In other words, God provides us with ideas so that we may prosper.

However, bread does not mean just food or material blessings alone. It also refers to "truth," "teaching," and "understanding." God's Truth gives us an understanding of life, of ourselves, and of others. God has truly given us "bread from heaven" so that we may have insight and understanding from day to day.

When Jesus was out in the desert wrestling with negative ideas, he repudiated the first temptation

3. See George M. Lamsa, *Old Testament Light,* a commentary based on the Aramaic Peshitta Text, Prentice-Hall, Inc., Englewood Cliffs, NJ, 1964, pp. 555-556.

with the words of the great Hebrew lawgiver. Matthew's gospel records Jesus' reply to the negative thought: "It is written that it is not by bread alone a human being lives but by every word that comes from the mouth of God" (Mt. 4:4). Moses first spoke these words, and he said, "Human beings cannot live by bread alone; but by everything that comes out of the mouth of *Yahweh* does a human being live" (Deut. 8:3).

Moses teaches us that material things *alone* cannot totally satisfy all human beings. Truth and guidance that come directly from God are also important to humans. When we follow God's law, our heavenly Father directs us to the appropriate channels of His supply. Through the Source of all supply, our material necessities are provided.

Material wealth alone will not bring equality, justice, and social order. Moses understood that having abundant wealth, without having the words which come from God's mouth—Truth and justice—would eventually lead to violence, chaos, and a disintegrating world. If we would have order in our social world, we must first have order within ourselves. Love and Truth with justice and equality come only through inner harmony of soul and spirit.

> And one of them who knew the law, asked him testing him: "Teacher, which is the greatest commandment in the law?" Now Jesus said to him: "You shall love the Lord your God with all your heart and with all your being and with all your power and

with all your mind. This is the greatest and first commandment. And the second, which is similar to it, is: 'You shall love your neighbor as yourself.' In these two commandments is the meaning of the Torah and the Prophets."

—Matthew 22:35-40

All These Things

We certainly cannot live without the necessities of life. But when we think only of material things and neglect our spiritual development, we lose our way. We may strive, at times, in erroneous and harmful ways, to obtain material things. In such cases, it is not the things themselves that are wrong, but the way in which we obtain them. However, by maintaining our spiritual focus and system of values based on spiritual insight, we will obtain in good and rightful ways the necessary things of life. This is what the Teacher from Galilee meant when he taught that we are to seek first the kingdom of God. "But first you search for the kingdom of God and his justice and all these things [material things] shall abundantly be given to you" (Mt. 6:33).

Our heavenly Father knows the things we need, and God supplies all that is good for us. God is "the Source and the Supply." All other sources are only channels through which God's inexhaustible supply flows. And God provides daily as is necessary.

Nature Always Provides

According to the first chapter of Genesis, the creation account, humans did not come on the scene until the sixth day of creation. God had provided everything before humans appeared on the earth. Food, shelter, and the necessities of life were all created first, in preparation for human beings. The earth was then ready to take care of humanity.

Nature always provides for its many species. But each species must look for and appropriate for its use nature's generous provision. However, we humans often think we need more than nature provides. Or we may suffer from thoughts of lack, such as, "There isn't enough to go around." Greed and unnecessary, excessive accumulation of wealth for tomorrow have proved an imbalance in our world.

Wealth

Wealth is good for all when it is circulated and properly shared. But there must be proper circulation to maintain it. Wealth must be *circulated*, not just *accumulated,* if it is to grow. When we hoard money, things, or whatever, we will lose them. By hoarding, we block the flow of good *from* us and *to* us. Our fear of lack sets up a *lack vibration* that attracts to us the very thing we fear.

Circulation is the positive action that keeps good flowing to all people, including ourselves. God has always provided for the human family. The apostle Jacob (James) says, "Every good and flawless gift is from above, and comes from the Father of lights, in whom there is no variation nor shadow of change" (Jas. 1:17).

The Fifth Attunement

Our Father has given us the intelligence and understanding to discover new and hidden resources for the betterment of humanity. All that any human being needs has already been provided for him or her. It is spiritual guidance within us that brings about all things properly, with good to all and harm to none. With this kind of realization, we can know that all is well. Let us tune in to the Source of all good, and our Supply will not fail us. This is the fifth attunement.

Chapter Eight
The Power of Forgiveness

Washwok-lan haubain akana dap hnan shwaqan l'hayawein—"Forgive us our offenses, as we have forgiven our offenders." Another way to translate the verse is this: "Free us [from] our offenses as also we have freed our offenders." We may also render the phrase: "Untie or release us [from] our offenses...."

Haubain, which literally means "debts," is peculiar to the Aramaic language in its own Semitic, early Palestinian context. Here in the prayer, the term "debt"—*hauba*—is a metaphor for "sin," "error," "guilt," "fault," "offense," "mistake," and "transgression." And the word *hayawein* literally signifies "debtors" but denotes "sinners," "offenders," and "transgressors." We also find this peculiar use of the Aramaic term *hauba* ("debt") for "sin," and "guilt" in the Dead Sea Scrolls. Interestingly, the word "sin," *hataya* in Aramaic, means "to miss" or "to miss the mark," thus a "mistake."

Shwaqan, which usually translates as "forgive" and "pardon," has other meanings. It denotes "to free," "to remit," "to untie," "to loosen," and "to release." With the distinctive Aramaic term meaning "debt," *shwaqan* carries the idea of "remittance," that is, "freeing and canceling" the debt.

Forgiveness Frees Us

Forgiveness frees us from past errors which we have committed or which have been committed against us. It enables us to begin on a new path of life. Sincere and genuine forgiveness heals any hurts or wrongs. Forgiveness strengthens the disheartened soul who has lost his or her way. It renews and refreshes our trust and faith in ourselves and in others. When we forgive, we are born again and become like a child. Through forgiveness we regain the precious attitude of an open and willing mind that is ever ready to learn anew.

Nature Does Not Condemn

Jesus was an earnest and zealous advocate of forgiveness. The central theme of Jesus' message was "the kingdom," but the second most important teaching concerned forgiveness. This is what makes his *gospel,* which in Aramaic means "joyful message," universally appealing and so powerful. He knew, through his own experiences of life and study of Scripture, that nature does not blame nor "point its finger" when things go wrong.

Nature always attempts to heal or correct an injury or hurt. For instance, if we should cut one of our fingers, immediately the life forces in the body rush to the aid of the injured area. These healing forces will fight off infection and start the coagulation of the blood to prevent excessive bleeding. The body does not attempt to search out the one who did the hurt and damage. Its only interest is to repair the injury.

When the physical form has been cut or hurt in any way, it doesn't ask: "Did you cut yourself by accident? Or did you do it deliberately?" And it is not going to say, "Well, if you cut yourself with the intention of hurting yourself, I am not going to heal you." The body is only concerned with healing the wound.

Jesus knew that God is a loving, forgiving Father. And, as a father, God cares for His children. He also knew that forgiveness was the only way to begin the rectification of human mistakes. Blaming doesn't heal anything, but pardoning does.

The Master Teacher, understanding humankind as he did, made room for human weaknesses and faults. Thus, he stressed the need to practice forgiveness. He was well acquainted with the powerful antidote that forgiveness holds for the human heart. Jesus knew that only the power of forgiveness could heal and restore broken and shattered relationships.

A Two-Way Street

"And free us from our offenses." How we all enjoy this part of the prayer! We all want to be free of guilt that usually accompanies past offenses. But there is a catch to this phrase, and it is this: "as also, we have released our offenders." How often we overlook this important part!

We surely appreciate being free from our offenses. And we also want others to put up with our shortcomings. But how well do we put up with the shortcomings of others? How tolerant and patient are we?

When we say this line of the prayer, we are asking, "Let me experience the same freedom from my errors and defects as I have allowed others to experience." Let's pause and think about this idea for a moment. How often have I heard many individuals say with all good intentions "I forgive him" or "I forgive her," and then a few minutes later these individuals begin a tirade against the so-called "forgiven one." In reality, they haven't released the offense. They're still holding on to the hurt and clinging to the idea that he or she needs to pay. They feel that there is a "debt" that one must pay!

When we hold grudges and allow them to build up in our minds and hearts, we suffer emotionally, mentally, and physically. Sometimes we become unbearable to live with. How can we expect forgiveness to be extended to us if we do not practice forgiveness?

If we become difficult and unforgiving toward others, they will treat us similarly. It is impossible to escape the law of reaping what we have sown. It is also perplexing for us when others may reflect back to us what we really think about ourselves. This reflection that returns to us from others appears as their *impression* of us. But, in reality, it is our own thinking coming back to haunt us.

It is essential for all concerned that we learn to practice forgiveness. It is healthy to forgive others and ourselves. Let us keep in mind that whatever mental or emotional message we send to others, we always keep the original thought, picture, and energy. The impression is made on our brain cells first before we can send it out. The chemical, electrical, and emotional forces build within us in a matter of seconds, be they good or bad.

Remember, what we send out is only a copy. We are the generators within the towers that beam out the signals. If we project hate and resentment toward others, we always keep the first and authentic pattern of these powers because we are the source. This also holds true when we project love, acceptance, and forgiveness. It takes a great deal of energy to stir up the forces of anger and resentment. But forgiveness causes joy, peace, and tranquility to flow through every cell in our bodies.

How Does One Let Go and Forgive?

Usually, it is difficult to forgive because we feel our emotions running wild throughout our bodies. Anger is a powerful emotional energy, and it needs a proper channel or outlet through which it can flow. Anger is a basic human emotion. No one escapes feeling its power. It is universal. It is very important to learn how to appropriately express anger so that it does not hurt us or others.

When I speak of anger, I do not refer to petty irritations that commonly plague us all. However, it is helpful if we can work with our irritations and anger when they are little and not so significant. Yet, there are times when anger builds to such an extent that it becomes totally unhealthy.

When I practiced pastoral counseling, many would come to me during the volcanic, eruptive stage of their anger. Commonly, I would sit and listen to the rage along with their intermittent apologies for carrying on with such volatile speech. Letting the anger out is one way of releasing the energy.

If, after the "bloodletting," one still focuses on the problem and continues with the anger, then it is no longer just the emotional energy at work. It is the thought process now that keeps the emotion of anger fueled. Disturbing and troubling thoughts need dismantling. This is one way of letting go.

There is also another way of letting go and forgiving. When we have thoroughly exhausted ourselves with our resentments, then the inner, godly, spiritual forces, which are present but usually dormant within us, can spring up. And we quickly discover there is more to us than we originally thought. We find that the power of love which appears to be beyond us has always been within us and does heal.

Sometimes, the ones we wish to forgive don't care if we forgive them or not. (This makes it even worse!) But, when love heals us, it doesn't matter what others may think or feel. It does not matter even if they don't accept our forgiveness.

In reality, forgiveness is really for ourselves. When we release others, we truly release the hurt and pain within our own emotional states. We are the ones carrying the resentment, and we pay for it. If someone has wronged us and we cannot do anything about it, why should we pay twice?

"Letting go and putting God first in our lives" means we would rather live with joy and peace within ourselves than live with resentment and bitterness. It is not healthy living when we harbor rancor and outrage. Neither is there any joy when we sublimate our feelings or when we want to retaliate. (Retaliation may bring joy to some individuals, but it is not lasting.) We are far better off when we "let go" of the problem. Recognizing and acknowledging the forgiving powers of one's inner Self is more rewarding. Let us right now let go and release all hurts and offenses! We can do it!

Wise as Serpents

However, forgiveness does not mean that we should lie down and let others walk all over us. Nor does it mean that we are not to be aware of certain individuals who are determined to hurt and create disharmony. Jesus told his disciples to "be wise as serpents." "Behold I am sending you like lambs among wolves; so be wise like snakes and innocent like doves" (Mt. 10:16). In simple language, *be smart or shrewd!*

When a snake is in danger, it coils and keeps its head in the center of the coil. The serpent does this so that it may protect its head. "Be wise as snakes" means "be shrewd; guard your faith, which protects you." Be aware of adversaries, but do not fear them.

Jesus used this saying because he observed nature. He knew that when a serpent sees trouble coming, it removes itself from the path. It wants to avoid being stepped on. Let us do the same thing.

When we see trouble coming, let's get out of the way, that is, sidestep it. Be wise when we know that someone wants to do evil and wishes to hurt. We can forgive them, but stay out of their way lest they "trample and crush" us.

Innocent as Doves

In the scriptural passage just mentioned above, Jesus also told his disciples to be "innocent as doves." Doves enjoy going where people are gentle and kind. They enjoy sitting on the shoulders of meek individuals. These birds make their nests in certain homes where they know they will receive no mistreatment. Doves can sense where there is peace and tranquility. In the Near East, people love to have them nearby. There is a reference to this phenomenon in the *Tanakh* (Old Testament). "The flowers appear on the earth; the time of pruning has come, and the voice of the turtle dove is heard in our land."[1]

The King James version of the Bible translates "turtledove" as "turtle." But the voice of the turtle cannot be heard. However, the voice of the turtledove is a joy to all. Hearing this voice means that doves have built a nest nearby; peace and tranquility reign.

When people become very upset and there is quarreling in the homes, the doves will leave. They become frightened at the vibrations they feel from the bickering and troublesome noises coming from these homes. But when they remain, it is a sign of peace and harmony.

Being "innocent as doves," we maintain a forgiving but wise heart. We will not remain where there is constant strife or where troublemakers dwell. We put love first in our lives and live in peace as much as we can. Let us avoid unnecessary conflicts and contentions whenever and wherever possible.

---

1. Song of Solomon 2:12, Aramaic Peshitta text, Lamsa translation.

Self-Forgiveness

There is something more to consider about the practice of forgiveness. Yes, Jesus does teach us through this line of the prayer that our forgiveness comes by forgiving others. And as we forgive others, we learn to forgive ourselves. People who refuse to forgive others usually won't forgive themselves either.

Then sometimes the opposite is true. We may find it easier to forgive others than to forgive ourselves. We can be very hard on ourselves but more lenient and considerate toward others. Learning to feel compassion for ourselves is just as important as forgiving others. Self-compassion aids us in practicing self-forgiveness. This is vital if we are to maintain a healthy, wholesome life. Let us realize and accept ourselves as we are, knowing that only through the fertile ground of self-compassion can we grow and find self-acceptance.

Pure in Heart

Meditating with our hearts on the power of forgiveness, we tune into the needs of others and to our own needs. Forgiveness assists us to clear and purify our minds and hearts of hatred and resentment. In this way we may commune with one another in joy and peace and with our heavenly Father. Jesus said, "Delighted are those who are pure in their hearts for they shall see God" (Mt. 5:8). Yes, we live in delight perceiving God's presence, when our hearts and minds are clear. *Pure in heart* is an Aramaic expression that means "a sincere person with a clear conscience."

The Sixth Attunement

Forgiveness revitalizes our hearts and emotions. It releases any inner tensions and bondages that may plague our minds and souls. We release others, and we release ourselves. We live in self-compassion and self-acceptance. Knowing this vital truth, we live in contentment, not needing the approval of others for self-acceptance.

This attunement would not be complete without the powerful act of forgiveness. We trap the inner powers of our souls to free others and ourselves. This is our sixth attunement.

Chapter Nine
Dealing With Materialism

Wla ta-alan l'nisyona ella pasan min beesha: "And do not let us enter into temptation, but deliver us from evil (error)." Most English translations of this verse read, "And do not *lead* us into temptation ...." Other translations read, "And do not *bring* us to the test ...." The idea is "Keep me out of trouble" or "Prevent me from *entering* harmful circumstances."

Benjamin Franklin
Interestingly, Benjamin Franklin, like many others of his time, was perplexed by this line of the prayer in the King James Version of the New Testament. So he decided to "modernize" it. His version of this phrase reads, "And keep us out of tempta- tion ...." As far as we know, Benjamin Franklin did not know the Aramaic language, yet he caught the idea behind this phrase of the prayer.

Benjamin Franklin, along with many other founding fathers of our nation, was a Deist. Deism originally was interchangeable with the term Theism. It means belief in one Supreme Being.

Deism as a belief was opposed to Atheism and Polytheism. Later in history, the term came to mean a system of natural religion. This was developed in England around the late 17th and 18th centuries.

Finally, this form of Deism developed the idea that the Supreme Being was totally transcendental. Then, later on, it splintered into various beliefs.

When Benjamin Franklin created his version of the prayer, he made two columns. One he labeled "Old Version," which was the King James Version, and the other he named "New Version" by Ben Franklin. He also annotated his rendition of the prayer and explained why he made the changes. The following is Ben Franklin's "New Version" of the prayer in its entirety:

Heavenly Father,
May all revere thee,
And become thy dutiful children
and faithful subjects.
May thy laws be obeyed on earth,
as perfectly as they are in heaven.
Provide for us this day, as thou
has hitherto daily done.
Forgive us our trespasses, and enable
us to forgive those who offend us.
Keep us out of temptation[1] and deliver
us from evil.
Amen.[2]

God Tempts No One

God never leads anyone into temptation nor tempts anyone! We know that God is *light*, *life*, and

---

1. The italics are not in the original version of Franklin's rendition of the Lord's Prayer. I have added them to make the comparison.

2. See John M. Haverstick, *The Progress of the Protestant: A Pictorial History From the Early Reformers to Present-Day Ecumenism*, Holt, Rinehart and Winston, New York, 1968, p. 128.

love. How can light lead into darkness? The Truth is that light always dispels darkness! We know that darkness cannot overcome or conquer light.

New Testament writers tell us that God is *love*. And love does not tempt us to do evil. God, as a loving and guiding parent, would not lead His children into darkness or temptation.

How would we feel if our children said to us, "Dad, Mom, don't lead us into temptation." How would we feel if they said this to us every day? What kind of parents would we be? No, our children know that we want to lead them away from trouble and temptation. This also holds true of our heavenly parent we call *abba*, Father.

Our inner spiritual energies are not going to lead us into temptation. Our own desires draw us into temptation. The apostle Jacob (James) in his epistle confirms this idea when he writes:

> When someone is tempted, don't say that he is tempted by God; because God cannot be tempted by evil, nor does he tempt anyone: But each one is tempted by his own desire; he covets and is seduced.
> —James 1:13-14

The Meaning of *Ta-alan*

The word *ta-alan* derives from the Aramaic root *al*. This root has many meanings. *Al* as a verb denotes "to enter," "to attack," "to fight," "to wrestle," and "to contend." It also means "to have intercourse." When the root *al* appears as a preposition, it can signify "on," "in," "by," "upon," "over," "above," "alongside," or "on top of." As you can see, one has to be very careful when translating this word either as a verb or a preposition.

In this phrase of the prayer, *ta-alan* means "to enter." Thus, the line correctly reads, "Do not let us *enter into* temptation." Jesus used the same word when he told his apostles, "Wake up and pray, that you may not enter (*ta-alon*) into temptation" (Mt. 26:41). Here, in this passage of Scripture, the verb form differs from the line in the prayer. In this verse the verb says *ta-alon* which means "that you may not enter" instead of *ta-alan*—"Let us not enter."

Temptation—Materialism

The Aramaic word *nisyona* carries the meaning of "tests," "trials," and "temptations." This word also carries another significance. Its nuance connotes "materialism" or "worldliness." Temptations and trials come from materialism or worldliness. When we say "Do not let us enter into materialism," we are really asking "Do not let us become deceived by the materialistic way of life."

This does not mean that we are to avoid using material things. What it signifies is that we are not to lose ourselves in materialistic things. Our lives need not center on material substance. God will provide what we need.

Nevertheless, materialism often dominates our thinking. Because of this, we lose sight of the spiritual principles that lie behind the material effects and objects we see. When we recognize only the effect (materialism) and not the spiritual principle of supply, we lose our balance. We are not seeing the Truth behind the material world. Through this insight of the prayer, then, we come to understand that it is important to keep a balance between spiritual principle and material manifestation.

Part Us—Deliver Us

Pasan indicates "part us," "separate us," "set us free," and not just "deliver us." The word *deliver* does not carry the full impact of the original Aramaic term. We don't want just to be "delivered" once we are involved in a situation. We want to be "parted" or "separated" from trouble before we become trapped or ensnared by it. Being guided away from the snare ahead of time helps us avoid complications that usually develop once we become trapped. The idea is to "keep us alert so that we do not enter the temptation" and "Set us free from erroneous thinking and actions that lead us into more problems and evils"—"Part us from error."

Evil or Error?

Beesha—evil has many subtle shades of meaning in the Aramaic language. It comes from the root word *beesh*, "to err," "to displease," "to harm," "to be evil," "to seem bad," "to mistake," "to afflict," "to be unripe," "to be immature," and "to be unfortunate." This word truly has a host of meanings. I have given only a few of the connotations. One has to know the context to translate the proper significance of the word.

The word *beesha* as a noun, adjective, or adverb has literally scores of various meanings. Here are some more meanings from this word: "bad," "ugly," "error," "cruel," "mistake," "malignant," "rotten," "unripe," "immature," "unfortunate," "unlucky," "wicked," "wrong," "diseased," "incorrect," "culprit," "deceiver," "troublemaker," and "the evil one." We can obtain a clearer understanding of this word by looking into a prophecy that the prophet Jeremiah spoke. In his vision the prophet sees two baskets of figs—one basket with good figs and the other with evil figs:

> And Yahweh said to me: "What do you see, Jeremiah?" And I replied: "Figs, good figs, very good; and evil figs, very evil, no one can eat them because they are so evil."
> —Jeremiah 24:3

Let us retranslate the verse with the proper meaning:

> And Yahweh said to me: "What do you see, Jeremiah?" And I replied: "Figs, ripe figs, very ripe figs; and unripe figs, very sour, no one can eat them because they are so sour."

We might wonder what the figs ever did to be "evil." They did nothing! The word as it appears in this passage simply means that they were sour or rotten, not edible. In the Near East, when people eat a fruit which is sour, they say, "this fruit is evil."

Jesus calls trees good (healthy) and bad (sick or unhealthy). He also says that fruits are good (ripe or edible) and bad (unripe or inedible). (See Mt. 7:17.) Again in another verse of Scripture, Jesus seems to suggest (according to most English translations) that although parents are evil, they know how to give good gifts to their children. Literally translated it says, "If, then, you *who are evil ones* know how to give good things to your children, how much more shall your Father who is in heaven give good things to those who ask Him?" (Mt. 7:11 KJV) But the intended meaning in Aramaic is this: "And if, then, *you who make mistakes* know how to give proper gifts ...."

In this line of the prayer, the implied meaning is "error," or "mistake." However, some biblical authorities suggest the word means "evil one," that is, "Satan." If one chooses to interpret *beesha* as "the evil one," it would simply mean "an evil person." This bad person implies a liar, thief, or anyone who would mislead or do harm. It does not mean the devil or a supernatural being. There is only one Power in the universe—God, the good, and the compassionate.

An evil cosmic being does not create our trials, challenges, and problems. We create them ourselves. And we do so from inappropriate choices, ignorance, misunderstandings, emotional immaturity, false beliefs, and misleading philosophies and ideologies.

When we realize this fact, then we are on our way to healthier living. We do not blame ourselves. We are recognizing our role and responsibility. We have the ability to respond to Truth that abides within us. We respond to God, who is the source of life.

Only God Can Part Us From Error

Only God—the true, good, inherent spiritual power who is a living part of us all—can direct and separate us from evil or mistakes. When we depend on the inner, spiritual energies and forces (God) and not just on what our eyes see or on our physical desires alone, we can avoid many situations that ordinarily would throw or overtake us.

Material things are necessary, but they will mislead us if they become our ultimate goal. If this happens, we can easily numb ourselves to our innate spiritual forces. We then take dangerous shortcuts that inevitably lead us down a troublesome road.

God's Spirit always enables us to see the right way when we heed our inner guidance. And if we do make a mistake, God will guide us in our restoration. We can learn from our mistakes and then go on to new and better ways.

The Seventh Attunement

In this attunement let us not enter (become ensnared by or saturated with) materialism, but as we make our gains, part us from error that may hurt others and our own lives as well. Yes, we are to make gains and meet our needs. All gains need to circulate and not just accumulate. We know that the balance of the universe depends on the circulation of good that nature provides.

As we pray this phrase of the prayer, we awaken and call upon our inner spiritual energies and forces so that they may continually guide us. Material things come and go. These things do not guide us.

We are open to God's counsel. By so doing we avoid many mistakes and bring greater happiness to ourselves and others. This is the seventh attunement.

Chapter Ten
Power and Glory

Mitol ddeelakhee malkutha whaila wtishbohta: la-alam almeen. Amen.—"Because the kingdom, the power, and the glory belong to You: from all ages throughout all the ages. Amen." The term *amen* in Aramaic means "sealed in faithfulness." One may also translate the verse to read: "Yours are the kingdom (counsel), energy, song, and praise throughout all the ages. Sealed in faith, trust, and truth."

The Majestic Close

This prayer comes to a close by bringing in the majesty and energy of God's parental power in all its splendor. At the beginning of the prayer the approach was very simple. *Abba*—Father, we recall, is "papa" or "daddy" in Aramaic.[1] The idea of a loving, compassionate, approachable parent and not a far-off, unapproachable Potentate began this prayer. In other words, we approach God with the full realization and wonderful sense of total union with this invisible power and presence. We are the offspring of the Almighty, who is a loving parent.

Now, at the end of the prayer, we acknowledge the inexhaustible, majestic Source that makes possible the attunements which we have affirmed. "For

---

1. See Chapter 2, "Abba–Father," pp. 27-30 of this book, Chapter 3, "Set Apart," p. 45, and Chapter 4, "Heavenly Counsel," p. 55.

the kingdom, power, and glory belong to You" are words through which we express something like this: "Dad, we know we can carry out these attunements because You are our source. You have it all! Yours are the kingdom and counsel! Yours are the energy, song and praise, and the magnificence! It is all Yours! You have what it takes to provide all that we may need now and forever!"

When our children come to us and make their needs known, they ask because they *know* we will do our best to provide what they need. How much more so will God provide as our "heavenly parent" when we ask Him! In plain language, not only is there inner guidance present within us but also the source of power to rise and meet any situation. We know and acknowledge that God's counsel, power, and glory reside within us. Our eternal Source is ever present! We, of ourselves, can do nothing, but from the Source of all power, we can do all things!

The Everlasting Kingdom

The Aramaic expression *la-alam almeen* means "from all ages, throughout all the ages." Others translate the phrase as "world without end." God's kingdom as the source of our energy and glory remains ever constant throughout all the ages. It never changes!

We often think that one nation, kingdom, or individual has "the answer" for the world, but that is not true, as history has proven. At one time the Assyrian Empire ruled the world. Then came the Babylonian (Chaldean) rule. After the Chaldeans, the Persians, then the Greeks, and the once great and imperial Roman Empire dominated the world. Where are these great powers today?

During the collapse of the Roman Empire, the Saracen movement rose in the Near East. Finally, moving closer to our day, the Ottoman Empire began to dominate. Then, the British Commonwealth spread its wings over the world. Today other great nations are in power, but for how long? Yet, in spite of all these colossal kingdoms, there has been and will always be "the kingdom" that human minds cannot manipulate. This kingdom is always in God's hands. It is forever and ever. We are never the Source, but we are the expression of this Source.

All nations rise and fall. No human kingdom on the face of the earth survives from ages to ages, from everlasting to everlasting. Only one kingdom endures throughout all the ages—God's universal kingdom! This is why we acknowledge "for thine is the kingdom" that never ends. God doesn't change. This spiritual Source is the same from ages to ages. It is we who awaken to this everlasting Source that is present for every generation!

Eternal Power and Glory

Haila in Aramaic signifies "power." It also denotes "might," "energy," "force," "potency," and "strength." This word also carries the sense of "prevailing power—enabling power." As an aside, the Aramaic expression *bar-haila*, literally "son of power," means "a soldier."

The Aramaic term *tishbohta* means "glory," "praise," "honor," and "magnificence." Liturgically, it refers to a "song," "hymn," or "chant." Its Aramaic root *shwh* denotes "to praise," "to glorify," "to honor," "to magnify," and "to celebrate."

If we and all nations would only give glory to the invisible Source and Creator of our universe, instead of aspiring just to our own glory, there would not be this need for world dominion. Nations fight over boundaries and land. Earth does not belong to us but it does belong to the One who created everything. Land is for the use of the entire human family.

All power and glory belong to our heavenly Father, who wants good for all His children. To the Creator, no one nation is greater or better than another. God's guidance is equal for all nations—"... so that you may be the children of your Father who is in heaven, he who lets his sun shine upon the good and upon the bad, and who lets his rain fall upon the just and the unjust" (Mt. 5:45).

Whether we speak of a nation or of an individual, each is unique, and each contributes to life in his or her own particular way. Every race and every nation contributes something of value to the whole of humankind. All good things come directly from our Father's counsel and guidance. This blesses all of us. It is through our Father's universal Counsel— God's kingdom, power, and glory that good reigns for everyone.

Therefore, we give all the might, power, and strength with songs and praise to our Creator. In other words, we complete our prayer and meditation with a thankful heart. We are full of joy and of thanks to the Creator of us all. We are full of praise and songs. A thankful person is a contented soul who lives in the joyful stream of gratefulness.

Science and Religion

Advancing in technology does not mean we have also advanced in our spiritual, religious understanding. In terms of religion, it appears we are standing still instead of moving forward. Today we have lost much of the true sense of religion as a soul science. (*Soul* means Being.) This world accomplishes much with technology but little in the field of religion that nurtures the soul.

Almost two thousand years have passed, and still Jesus' teachings are not properly understood nor are they implemented. And those teachings that we have understood we usually do not practice. Part of the problem is that we have become too bogged down in outward forms of religion. Religious trappings appear to be more important than the heart of religion. Dogmas and creedal uniformity also weigh heavily in our hearts and minds instead of the original teachings of Jesus.

However, today more than ever, we have the opportunity to plumb and explore the depths of our souls. As we open ourselves to divine counsel and guidance in its many expressions, we can make great strides and progress in the religion of the soul. Let us begin right now trapping and expressing all the good that we are.

A Commitment

The prayer closes with the Aramaic word *amen*. It means "to make firm" and refers to anything that is true, lasting, never-ceasing, eternal, perpetual, continual, and faithful. As a name, *ameena* refers to a "faithful one," "truthful one," and "sincere person." Interestingly, the Aramaic words for "believe" and "faith" derive from the root *amen*. So, believing and having faith denote standing firm.

Amen means so much more than just "So it is" or "So be it," though *amen* carries those meanings. When we say *amen* to our prayers, we declare that we will back up and stand by what we have just prayed. We will be faithful to our commitment in prayer.

Oral Contracts

In Jesus' day when businessmen made contracts, they did not make written agreements. They made their arrangements orally. When they completed their oral contract, they would say "amen" to each other. Both parties were saying to each other, "I'll keep my side of the bargain." The parties involved knew that they must be faithful to their oral agreement and carry out everything they had agreed to do.

When using the word *amen*, it means "I am committed; I'll be faithful." With the word *amen,* we are acknowledging our willingness to work with that which we have prayed, declared, and affirmed. We are confident in our conviction that we will receive our requests. And if not, we know that "No" is also a positive answer. Let us remember that spiritual forces only work for our good. So, let us be confident when we ask. "Anything you pray for and ask, be confident (believe) that you will receive it, and it will be done for you" (Mt. 11:24).

The Final Attunement

Knowing that God, as our loving parent, cares for us and wants only good for us, we can rest assured that He will keep His part of the agreement. God never changes. Therefore, we, also, shall be faithful to our part of the prayer.

Through this attunement we fill our hearts and minds with beneficial mental and emotional assurances. We are one with the inexhaustible Source—God's unending supply that is ever present within us and existing around us. We recognize and feel divine guidance in all its power and glory flowing through us and out from us. We stand firm in this truth. Amen!

Walking the Path—A Summary

God as loving, infinite Intelligence is everywhere and is through everything. "Setting a trap for God" is the ancient meaning of the word *prayer*. We can trap all the love, spirit, joy, peace, truth, energy, and compassion we need when we are open and receptive to all the good there is for us.

In reality, prayer is an attitude of spirit and mind that prepares us to receive. It enables us to receive God's provision and to express our thanks and our gratitude. God's presence is what brings health and power into our lives.

Spiritual energies working in our souls can and do solve our difficulties. It doesn't matter whether the trials or challenges exist in our homes, relationships, or finances. Universal forces never work against us. These spiritual powers that dwell within us always guide and help us. The only condition is that we trap and work with the universal program and not our own agenda.

The Path of Wholeness

As we have now seen, the counsel to pray "in Jesus' name" means that we are to pray *in the same awareness and consciousness* in which he prayed. His communion with the Father was of intimacy and perception. He did not beg and plead in prayer but acknowledged the power of prayer. Jesus attuned himself to the reality that one feels and knows while communing with spiritual forces.

When we understand this simple and direct prayer and are truly attuned to its meaning, then our attitude will be in harmony with infinite Intelligence. Our actions will naturally and spontaneously evidence our inner attunement with the spiritual presence we call God.

Setting the Trap

Jesus of Nazareth gave these instructions for prayer:

As for you, when you pray, enter your inner room[2] and lock your door and pray privately to your Father; and your Father who secretly watches shall pay you openly. And when you are praying, be not babbling like the pagans; for they are expecting that through the abundance of words they will be heard. Thus, do not be like them; for

2. The word for "room" in Aramaic is *tawanaah.* It refers to a room without windows, a closet, or a room in which supplies and valuables may be stored. *Inner room* in this verse is a metaphor meaning "heart or mind."

your Father knows what you need, before
you ask Him. Now you pray *this way*!
—Matthew 6:6-9

The phrase "Now you pray *this way*" means "to
pray something like this" or "in this manner," and
not necessarily *to pray in these exact words*. The
lines of this prayer are suggestions that are aligned
with essential Truth. They contain ideas that attune
us to God's program (the universal program) for the
entire human family. When we pray, we pray with
the basic thoughts of the Lord's Prayer in mind and
not the precise words. Although one may pray using
the words recorded in Matthew's gospel, there is
nothing wrong in repeating the Lord's Prayer.

The Attunements

• We realize and acknowledge who God is—a
loving Parent who is ever present, everywhere guiding and caring for all His children.

• We realize and acknowledge who we are—children of a gracious Father who provides in all ways
for the human family.

• We realize and work with God's sovereign
counsel moving within our hearts and minds. We
know that the kingdom is present everywhere for all
humanity.

• We realize and acknowledge God's desire (will)
for all of us to be healthy and to live in peace and
prosperity.

• We realize and acknowledge it is God who provides our daily supply so that we need not fear the future.

• We realize and acknowledge the value of forgiveness for ourselves and others.

• We realize and acknowledge our divine Source within, leading us away from trouble. We know that God continually separates us from error. He ever guides us in Truth.

• We realize and acknowledge that the kingdom, power, and glory all belong to an invisible Source and Presence we call God—our Father.

• We realize and acknowledge that this kingdom (counsel), power, and glory are from everlasting to everlasting for all generations.

• We realize and acknowledge that there is only one Presence, Kingdom, Power, and Glory everywhere, from all ages, thoughout all ages!

• We recognize and acknowledge our ability to respond to these realizations. We seal this prayer in faith, trust, and Truth. We stand behind these prayerful words, for all these powers and energies are natural to our beings.

Epilogue

Trapping God simply means working with our own God-given innate physical, mental, and spiritual energies. Aramaic Scripture tells us that "God is not a man that he should lie; neither a human being that he should be given counsel" (Num. 23:19). The standard version says, "God is not a man, that he should lie; neither the son of man, that he should repent" (Num. 23:19 KJV).

God is not a man! We really do not know what God is. Many have attempted to define God but it is impossible to fully conceptualize what God is.[3] We can feel God and sense through our hearts only certain aspects of God, but that is all.

Jesus describes God as a loving parent, a father who cares for and guides His beloved children (humankind). But, he also describes God as a caring shepherd continually seeking those who, like sheep, may stray and healing those who may be injured, bruised, or ill. These are all conceptual, yet intimate, ideas about God.

God is beyond functional thought but not beyond human consciousness or the sensitivity of the human soul. Many deep experiences in life are extremely difficult to define or capture with words alone. For example, love defies definition. There exist certain realizations that occur in the human heart and consciousness which cannot be fully comprehended, but which can be apprehended.

As human beings, we have the faculties to know and commune with God's presence and understand godly attributes because they are inherent within us. Thus, "setting a trap for God," which is the ancient meaning of prayer, allows us to realize our innate Godly energies of peace, love, and joy for our own benefit and for the benefit of others. We can and do trap God's essence and are able to work with this

3. See my book *The Mysteries of Creation: The Genesis Story,* Noohra Foundation, Santa Fe, 1993, pp. 49-59.

realization.

When we consciously realize this union within ourselves, our bodies themselves become the living temples of compassion and universal love. These words are not just ideas into which we are trying to fit ourselves. This would not work at all. These are tangible experiences of life itself working within our physical forms, healing us and others.

When we are devoted to higher harmony in life, we enter into a deeper understanding of self- knowledge. We then will nourish and cultivate our souls in the environment of God's presence—compassionate love that indwells us all. "In that day you will know that I am in my Father, and you are in me, and I am in you" (Jn. 14:20). "But you know him [the spirit of Truth] because he dwells with you and is in you" (Jn. 14:17).

Amen!

Bibliography

Black, Matthew, *Aramaic Approach to the Gospels and Acts*, 2nd ed. 1954, 3rd ed. 1967, Clarendon Press, Oxford, 1946.

Charlesworth, James H., *Jesus Within Judaism: New Light from Exciting Archaeological Discoveries*, Doubleday, New York, 1988.

Errico, Rocco A., *Let There Be Light: The Seven Keys*, Noohra Foundation, Santa Fe, New Mexico, 1994.

_____, *The Message of Matthew: An Annotated Parallel Aramaic-English Gospel of Matthew*, Noohra Foundation, Irvine, California, 1991.

_____, *The Mysteries of Creation: The Genesis Story*, Noohra Foundation, Santa Fe, New Mexico, 1993.

Haverstick, John M., *The Progress of the Protestant: A Pictorial History From the Early Reformers to Present-Day Ecumenism*, Holt, Rinehart and Winston, New York, 1968.

Klausner, Joseph, *Jesus of Nazareth*, tr. Herbert Danby, Macmillan, New York, 1943.

Lamsa, George M., *Gospel Light*, A. J. Holman Co., Philadelphia, 1939.

_____, *Holy Bible From the Ancient Eastern Text*, A. J. Holman Co., Philadelphia, 1939.

_____, *More Light on the Gospel*, Doubleday and Co., Garden City, New York, 1968.

_____, *Old Testament Light*, Prentice-Hall, Inc., Englewood Cliffs, New Jersey, 1964.

Miller, John W., *Biblical Faith and Fathering: Why We Call God "Father,"* Paulist Press, New Jersey, 1989.

The New Testament, Peshitta Text, Classical Eastern (Assyrian-Chaldean) Aramaic script, Mosul, Baghdad, 1950.

Rihbany, Abraham M., *The Syrian Christ*, Houghton Mifflin Co., Boston, 1916.

Scott, Bernard Brandon, *Jesus, Symbol-Maker for the Kingdom*, Fortress Press, Philadelphia, 1981.

Tolstoy, Leo, *My Confession* (1879–1882) and *The Spirit of Christ's Teaching*, Walter Scott, London, n.d.

Zeitlin, Irving M., *Jesus and the Judaism of His Time*, Polity Press, Blackwell, Oxford, 1988.

About the Author

Rocco A. Errico is the founder and president of the Noohra Foundation of Santa Fe, New Mexico. (*Noohra* is an Aramaic word that means "light.") The Noohra Foundation is a nonprofit, nonsectarian, nondenominational, spiritual educational organization of Aramaic biblical studies, research, and publications. Dr. Errico is an ordained minister, lecturer, author, Bible authority, translator, Aramaic instructor, educator, and spiritual counselor.

For ten years he studied intensively with the late George M. Lamsa, Th.D., world-renowned Assyrian biblical scholar and translator of *Holy Bible From the Ancient Eastern Text*. Dr. Errico is proficient in Aramaic and Hebrew exegesis—Old and New Testaments—and in the customs, idioms, psychology, symbolism, and philosophy of Semitic peoples. He is also fluent in the Spanish language and has translated his book *The Ancient Aramaic Prayer of Jesus: The Lord's Prayer* into Spanish. He is also in the process of translating *The Gospel According to Matthew* from Aramaic into Spanish and his book *Let There Be Light: The Seven Keys* into Spanish.

Dr. Errico holds a doctorate in letters from the College of Seminarians (The Apostolic Succession of Antioch and the Church of the East—American See), a doctorate in philosophy from the School of Christianity, Los Angeles, a doctorate in divinity from St. Ephrem's Institute, Sweden, and a doctorate in sacred theology from the School of Christianity, Los Angeles. Dr. Errico also holds a special title of teacher, prime exegete (*Malpana d'miltha d'lahu*), among The Federation of St. Thomas Christians of the Order of Antioch.

He serves as a professor of biblical studies in schools of ministry for many denominations and is a regular feature writer for several religious publications. He formerly served as an editor and writer of *Light for All,* a religious magazine. He has held advisory positions with many boards of ecumenical religious organizations. Dr. Errico lectures extensively throughout the country and is widely known for his numerous radio and television appearances.

Under the auspices of the Noohra Foundation, Dr. Errico continues to speak to colleges, civic groups, and churches of various denominations.

Write the Noohra Foundation for a complimentary catalog of Aramaic Bible translations, books, audio- and videocassettes, and a brochure of classes, retreats, and seminars. Those interested in scheduling Dr. Errico for speaking engagements may also write to:

Noohra Foundation
4480 South Cobb Dr., Ste. H PMB 343
Smyrna, GA 30080-6989

Phone: (678) 945-4006

Email: *info@noohra.com*

www.noohra.com